weekend baking

weekend baking

easy recipes for relaxed family baking

RYLAND
PETERS
& SMALL

LONDON NEW YORK

Sarah Randell

photography by Kate Whitaker

Dedication
For my parents, for teaching me what good food is all about.

Design, Photographic Art Direction, and Prop Styling Steve Painter
Senior Editor Céline Hughes
Production Controller Toby Marshall
Art Director Leslie Harrington
Publishing Director Alison Starling

Food Stylist Joss Herd
Food Stylist's Assistants Tim Jenner and Laura Fyfe
Indexer Hilary Bird

First published in the US in 2010
by Ryland Peters & Small
519 Broadway, 5th Floor
New York, NY 10012
www.rylandpeters.com

10 9 8 7 6 5 4 3 2 1

Text © Sarah Randell 2010
Design and photographs
© Ryland Peters & Small 2010

Printed in China

ISBN: 978 1 84975 033 2

Author's acknowledgments

Thank you to the team at Ryland Peters & Small, plus Kate Whitaker and the lovely Joss for such gorgeous pics.

And, a special thank you to B, for tasting umpteen cakes with me, both the successes and the slightly doubtful, with unfaltering enthusiasm and always, with a smile, x.

Publisher's acknowledgments

For loan of props: Jane Wicks, Kitchenalia at 'Country Ways', Rye, East Sussex; Soendergaard Design for hand-thrown porcelain: soendergaarddesign.co.uk; Kitchenaid for the loan of the electric mixer in this book: www.kitchenaid.com for products and your nearest stockist.

The lovely Kitty for being the perfect child model.

Nuala McArdle for hair and make-up.

Steve Painter and Nuala McArdle for allowing us to use their home in Hastings for location photography.

Library of Congress Cataloging-in-Publication Data

Randell, Sarah.
  Weekend baking : easy recipes for relaxed family baking / Sarah Randell ; photography by Kate Whitaker.
    p. cm.
  Includes index.
  ISBN 978-1-84975-033-2
  1. Baking. 2. Desserts. I. Title.
  TX763.R24 2010
  641.8'15--dc22

                              2010022713

Notes

- All spoon measurements are based on measuring spoons and are level unless otherwise stated.
- Butter is salted, unless otherwise stated. If you need softened butter for a recipe, leave it at room temperature for several hours before you start. I leave it out of the refrigerator overnight if I am using it for baking the next day.
- All baking pan measurements given are base measurements. Use nonstick bakeware to avoid sticky moments.
- If you bake frequently, it is worth investing in reusable plastic baking liners to save on baking parchment.
- All eggs are large, unless otherwise stated. If possible, use eggs at room temperature.
- I use unrefined cane sugar. The flavors are more complex than refined sugars and enhance the final results. A word of warning though—unrefined confectioners' sugar isn't white, so although it can look gorgeous on some cakes, it may not always be the best option to use for frostings!
- Ovens should be preheated to the specified temperature. Recipes in this book were tested using a regular oven. If using a convection oven, follow the manufacturer's instructions for adjusting temperatures.

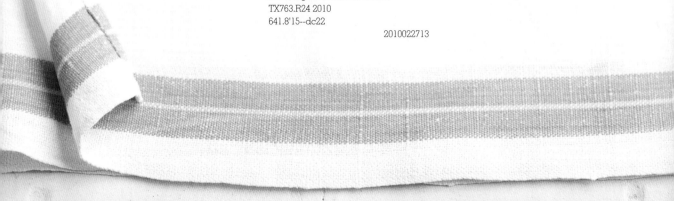

contents

Introduction

A day spent in the kitchen, mixing and baking, with the radio murmuring in the background is, to me, a day well spent. The warmth of the oven and the deliciously sweet, spicy, chocolatey, or citrussy smells that may waft from its tightly closed door are not only truly comforting but ultimately satisfying too. Whether it be a batch of buttery madeleines, a pan of fruit-packed muffins, some giant chocolate chip cookies, or a traditional chocolate layer cake for a birthday, I guarantee you will feel wonderfully smug and proud as they cool on a rack in the kitchen, waiting to be devoured or coated in a whipped icing or sticky glaze.

Children tend to be particularly enthusiastic about helping when it comes to baking. There are plenty of opportunities for little fingers to help measure, mix, and decorate, and then to show what they have made. I'm not suggesting that children should eat cake every day, nor that we adults should, but quiet interludes in the kitchen can be just as absorbing for them as for us and highly rewarding. The time it takes to bake a cake is, in my experience, as enjoyable as eating it.

If you are a beginner, there are lots of simple baking recipes here to tempt you. All you need is some time and a few basic tools. If you are buying new bakeware, I urge you to invest in some good-quality pans—it really will be worth it in the long run and will last for years. As for mixing, I have an electric mixer, which I use for nearly all my baking, but I used to rely on an electric hand whisk that I have now had for 20 years and it is still going strong. If you don't have anything similar, a mixing bowl and a balloon whisk or wooden spoon, accompanied by a bit of elbow grease, will usually suffice.

For more experienced cooks, there are some new ideas here to try and have fun with. Whatever takes your fancy, I hope sugar and spice become as big a part of your pantry in the future as they are mine. Happy baking.

small cakes

scones with strawberry jam and plenty of clotted cream

Scones are best eaten the day they are made, but they do freeze well if you have a few left over. Thick, luscious clotted cream is a specialty of Devon, England, for which there is no American equivalent. Look for clotted cream at gourmet stores.

1 large egg

about ½ cup milk

a squeeze of lemon juice

1¾ cups all-purpose flour

2 rounded teaspoons baking powder

2 tablespoons sugar, plus extra for sprinkling

a pinch of salt

3 tablespoons butter, softened and cubed

strawberry jam, to serve

clotted cream, to serve

a plain 2-in. cookie cutter

a baking sheet, oiled

Makes about 10

Preheat the oven to 425°F.

Put the egg and milk in a small bowl and lightly beat, then mix in the lemon juice.

Sift the flour and baking powder into a large mixing bowl and stir in the 2 tablespoons of sugar and the salt.

Scatter the cubes of butter over the flour mixture and, using a table knife, cut them into the flour. Now, lightly rub the butter into the flour, using your fingertips, until the mixture resembles bread crumbs.

Pour in half the egg mixture and, using the knife again, mix the liquid into the dry ingredients using a cutting action. Add as much of the remaining egg mixture as you need to, to be able to bring everything together into a dough—you probably won't need it all.

Tip the dough out onto a lightly floured work surface and gently pat it out until it is about 1 inch thick. Using the cutter, stamp out scones, then gently re-form the dough and continue until you have used it all.

Arrange the scones on the baking sheet. Brush the tops with any leftover egg mixture and sprinkle generously with sugar. Bake in the preheated oven for about 10–12 minutes, or until risen and golden.

Let the scones cool on a wire rack. Serve with generous amounts of jam and clotted cream to spread on the halved scones.

toffee pear muffins

The toffee in these muffins is dulce de leche: thick, luscious Argentinian caramel, sold in cans or jars. It also makes a delicious sauce to serve with sautéed pears, apples, or bananas, for a quick dessert, if you have some left over.

10 tablespoons butter

⅔ cup milk

3 large eggs

6 tablespoons dulce de leche

½ cup packed light brown sugar, plus extra for sprinkling

2⅓ cups self-rising flour

1 heaping teaspoon baking powder

2 rounded teaspoons apple pie spice

2 large, ripe but firm pears, cored, peeled, and chopped into small pieces

1 rounded tablespoon old-fashioned rolled oats

a 12-cup muffin pan, lined with paper muffin liners

Makes 12

Preheat the oven to 400°F.

Melt the butter in a small pan and let cool slightly.

In a large mixing bowl and using a balloon whisk, whisk together the milk, eggs, 2 tablespoons of the dulce de leche, the sugar, and the melted butter.

Sift in the flour, baking powder, and apple pie spice and whisk together. Scatter the chopped pear over the top and, using a large metal spoon, gently fold it in until just combined.

Spoon the batter (which will be quite sloppy) into the muffin liners. Sprinkle each muffin with a little extra sugar and a few oats. Bake the muffins in the preheated oven for 30–35 minutes, or until risen and lightly golden.

Let the muffins cool for 10 minutes or so, then, using a small, sharp knife, cut a small cross in the top of each muffin and spoon half a teaspoonful of dulce de leche into each one. Let it settle, then add another half a teaspoonful to sit on top. Eat while still warm.

chocolate heaven muffins

These muffins are bursting with chocolate and are as easy as pie to rustle up. For the ultimate chocolate experience, eat them fresh from the oven.

5 tablespoons butter

2½ oz. bittersweet chocolate (about 50% cocoa solids)

2½ oz. milk chocolate

2 oz. white chocolate

½ cup sour cream

3 tablespoons milk

¼ cup light muscovado or packed light brown sugar

2 large eggs

1⅓ cups all-purpose flour

2 tablespoons cocoa powder

1 tablespoon baking powder

a pinch of salt

1 tablespoon demerara sugar

a 6-cup muffin pan, lined with paper muffin liners

Makes 6

Preheat the oven to 400°F.

Melt the butter in a small pan and let cool slightly.

Chop the three types of chocolate into small chunks.

In a large mixing bowl and using a balloon whisk, whisk together the sour cream, milk, muscovado sugar, eggs, and melted butter.

Sift in the flour, cocoa, and baking powder. Sprinkle in the salt and add all the chopped chocolate. Using a large metal spoon, fold everything together until combined, but don't over-mix.

Spoon the batter into the muffin liners. Sprinkle each muffin with a little demerara sugar. Bake the muffins in the preheated oven for 20 minutes—by which time they will be risen, but still very slightly unset in the middle. They will continue to cook as they cool.

crunchy-topped raspberry and banana muffins

Delicious warm or cold, for breakfast or tea, these muffins are also ideal for packed lunches and they freeze well. Another time, use blueberries instead of the raspberries to ring the changes.

10 tablespoons butter

2 very ripe bananas

⅔ cup milk

¾ cup sugar

3 large eggs

2⅓ cups self-rising flour

1 slightly rounded teaspoon baking powder

1½ cups raspberries

3–4 tablespoons demerara sugar

2 tablespoons sunflower seeds

a 12-cup muffin pan, lined with paper muffin liners

Makes 12

Preheat the oven to 400°F.

Melt the butter in a small pan and let cool slightly.

Peel and mash the bananas.

In a large mixing bowl and using a balloon whisk, whisk together the milk, sugar, eggs, and melted butter.

Sift in the flour and baking powder and add the raspberries and banana. Using a large metal spoon, fold everything together until combined, but don't over-mix.

Spoon the batter into the muffin liners. Sprinkle each muffin with a little demerara sugar and the sunflower seeds. Bake the muffins for 30–35 minutes, or until risen and golden. Let cool on a wire rack.

blueberry lime friands

If you haven't come across friands before, you will soon be converted. They are based on the French teacakes called *financiers*. If you don't want to invest in a special friand pan, you can make these in a regular muffin pan.

1 stick butter

½ cup shelled, blanched whole hazelnuts

¾ cup confectioners' sugar

¾ cup all-purpose flour

finely grated peel of 2 limes

1⅜ cups blueberries

4 large egg whites

Lime syrup

freshly squeezed juice of 1 small lime

3 tablespoons sugar

a 9-cup friand pan, well buttered

Makes 9

Preheat the oven to 400°F.

Melt the butter in a small pan and let cool slightly.

Whiz the hazelnuts in a blender until finely ground.

Sift the confectioners' sugar and flour into a large mixing bowl. Stir in the ground hazelnuts, lime peel, and blueberries.

Put the egg whites in a large, scrupulously clean bowl and whisk until they form soft peaks.

Using a large metal spoon, fold half the egg whites into the flour mixture with half the melted butter—be as gentle as you can be. Fold in the other half of the egg whites and melted butter.

Spoon the batter into the cups of the prepared friand pan. Bake in the preheated oven for 20 minutes.

To make the lime syrup, heat the lime juice and sugar together in a small pan, stirring, until all the sugar has dissolved.

Let the baked friands cool for 5 minutes, then make a few holes in the top of each one using the point of a small, sharp knife. Drizzle a little of the lime syrup over each of the warm cakes, allowing it to seep into the holes. Leave the friands in the pan until completely cold, before running a knife around the edges and turning them out.

vanilla cupcakes with raspberry frosting

These cakes, with their pretty pink frosting, are ideal for little girls' birthday parties and a good recipe to make with children. If you want to turn these into grown-up cakes, use the same frosting, but top each one with a fresh raspberry.

1½ sticks butter, softened and cubed

¾ cup sugar

3 large eggs

1⅓ cups self-rising flour, sifted

3 tablespoons milk

1 teaspoon pure vanilla extract

tiny sugar balls, sprinkles, or pink edible glitter, to decorate

Raspberry frosting

5 tablespoons unsalted butter

⅔ cup raspberries

⅛ cup sugar

5 oz. cream cheese, chilled

a 12-cup muffin pan, lined with paper cupcake liners

Makes 10

Preheat the oven to 350°F.

Put the butter, sugar, eggs, and flour in an electric mixer (or use a large mixing bowl and an electric whisk). Whisk together for a few minutes to combine. Add the milk and vanilla and whisk again.

Spoon the batter into the cupcake liners. Bake in the preheated oven for 25–30 minutes, or until risen and golden. Let cool on a wire rack.

To make the raspberry frosting, melt the butter in a small pan and let cool slightly.

Put the raspberries in a separate small pan and heat up —just until they reach simmering point and become a seedy purée. Take the pan off the heat and tip the purée into a coarse strainer set over a small bowl. Strain the purée, let the juice cool, and discard the seeds.

Whisk together the sugar and cream cheese. Add the melted butter and whisk again. Finally, add 2 teaspoons of the cooled raspberry juice and mix again. You are aiming for a pretty pink color, so add more juice as necessary. Refrigerate the frosting until the cupcakes have completely cooled.

Top each cake with pink frosting—you can spread it on with a spatula, or use a piping bag, as you wish. Decorate with sugar balls, sprinkles, or edible glitter.

ginger meringues

Meringues really are easy to make and, if you want to get ahead, they will keep for a couple of days in an airtight container before sandwiching together.

3 large egg whites

a scant cup sugar

1 ball stem ginger in syrup, drained and very finely chopped

Ginger cream

⅔ cup heavy cream

1 ball stem ginger in syrup, drained and very finely chopped

2 baking sheets, lined with baking parchment (don't grease it, or your egg whites will collapse!)

Makes 15

Preheat the oven to 275°F.

Put the egg whites in a large, scrupulously clean bowl and whisk until they form stiff peaks. Now, gradually add the sugar—in tablespoonfuls—whisking all the time. You will end up with a smooth, thick, glossy meringue. Using a large metal spoon, gently fold in the chopped ginger.

Using a teaspoon, make 15 small mounds on each of the prepared baking sheets, swirling each mound into a peak using the end of a skewer. Each meringue should be about 2 inches in diameter at the base.

Bake in the preheated oven for 30 minutes, then turn off the oven and leave the meringues in the oven until completely cold, ideally overnight.

To make the ginger cream, whip the cream until it forms soft peaks, then stir in the chopped ginger. Use to sandwich the meringues together in pairs.

mini chocolate, beet, and cherry cakes

Using beets in these cakes gives them slightly soft, moist centers and they freeze well, before decorating. If you are making them as a gift, dust the tops with cocoa, then sprinkle with edible mini gold balls—dip the end of your finger in a little cold water before applying so that they stick.

2½ oz. bittersweet chocolate (about 50% cocoa solids)

⅓ cup dried sour cherries (or dried cranberries)

1⅓ cups self-rising flour

⅓ cup cocoa powder

¾ cup light muscovado or packed light brown sugar

1 cup peanut or vegetable oil

3 large eggs

a pinch of salt

5 oz. cooked, peeled beets

a 9-hole petite loaf pan (holes measuring 2½ x 3⅜ in. and 1½ in. deep), lined with paper mini-loaf liners

Makes 9

Preheat the oven to 350°F.

Break the chocolate into pieces and melt it in a heatproof bowl set over a pan of simmering water. Let cool slightly.

Roughly chop the sour cherries.

Sift the flour into an electric mixer (or use a large mixing bowl and an electric whisk). Add the cocoa, sugar, oil, eggs, salt, and the melted chocolate, and whisk until combined. Using the coarse side of a grater, grate the cooked beet into the mixture and sprinkle in the chopped sour cherries. Using a large metal spoon, fold everything together gently.

Spoon the batter into the loaf liners. Bake in the preheated oven for 20–25 minutes, or until well risen. Let the cakes cool completely in the pan.

Note: The petite loaf pan and matching liners needed for these cakes can be bought from www.wilton.com. If you prefer, you can bake the cakes in muffin liners instead of mini-loaf liners—they will take 25–30 minutes in the oven, and make 9 muffins.

honey and rosemary madeleines

I like to use eucalyptus or Greek honey to make these, as it partners well with the delicate flavor of the rosemary, but you can, of course, use your own favorite honey. If you want to keep things simple, they are equally delicious without the rosemary. Madeleines are best eaten fresh on the day of baking, but they do freeze well.

5 tablespoons butter

2 tablespoons honey

2 fresh rosemary sprigs

2 large eggs

⅓ cup sugar

⅓ cup self-rising flour

½ teaspoon baking powder

⅓ cup ground almonds

a small pinch of salt

a 12-hole madeleine pan, well buttered and lightly dusted with flour

Makes 18

Put the butter, honey, and sprigs of rosemary in a small pan over the lowest possible heat. Heat gently, giving it a swirl now and then. Take the pan off the heat and let the mixture cool and infuse for 15 minutes.

Put the eggs and sugar in an electric mixer (or use a large mixing bowl and an electric whisk) and whisk until pale and mousselike—this can take up to 10 minutes.

Preheat the oven to 400°F.

Sift the flour into a large mixing bowl and stir in the baking powder, almonds, and salt. Add half the melted butter mixture (removing the sprigs of rosemary as you do so) and half the flour mixture to the beaten eggs and sugar. Using a large metal spoon, fold everything together quickly but gently. Repeat this process with the remaining melted butter mixture and the flour mixture.

Fill the holes of the pan with mixture. Bake the madeleines in the preheated oven for 8–10 minutes, or until golden and risen. Let the madeleines cool in the pan for a couple of minutes, then remove (you may need a table knife to help ease them out) and transfer to a wire rack. Wash, re-grease, and re-flour the pan before baking the remaining batter. You should make 18 madeleines in total.

plum, orange, and double almond crumble tartlets

If you are not confident making pie crust, you shouldn't have any problems here, as this is a well-behaved crust recipe. These tarts can also be turned into mince pies for Christmas—just substitute the jam and plums with 3 cups of mincemeat.

Crust

1⅓ cups all-purpose flour

6½ tablespoons unsalted butter, softened

1 tablespoon confectioners' sugar, plus extra for dusting (optional)

1 large egg, lightly beaten

Crumble filling

⅛ cup demerara sugar

2 tablespoons unsalted butter, chilled and cubed

⅛ cup all-purpose flour

3 tablespoons rolled oats

1 heaping tablespoon slivered almonds

grated peel of 1 large orange (use a zester, if you have one, rather than a fine grater)

3 ripe but firm plums

2 tablespoons shelled almonds (skin on)

7–8 tablespoons plum jam, such as damson

a fluted 3½-in. cookie cutter

2 x 12-cup muffin pans, oiled

Makes 24

To make the crust, put the flour, butter, and confectioners' sugar in an electric mixer. Mix for a minute or until the mixture resembles bread crumbs. Add the egg and briefly mix again. As soon as the dough starts to come together, tip it onto the work surface and bring it together in a ball. Press the ball into a disc, wrap in plastic wrap, and refrigerate it for 30 minutes.

To make the crumble filling, briefly mix the sugar, butter, and flour in the electric mixer, again until the mixture resembles bread crumbs. Stir in the oats, slivered almonds, and orange peel.

On a lightly floured work surface, roll out the dough until it is about ⅛ inch thick. It may be easier to roll out half at a time. Using the cutter, stamp out rounds and use to line the cups of the pans—the dough will come about halfway up the side of each cup. Re-form and re-roll the dough, then keep stamping out rounds until you have 24. Refrigerate the dough-lined pans for 30 minutes.

Meanwhile, halve, pit, and chop the plums into pea-sized pieces. Roughly chop the whole almonds.

Preheat the oven to 400°F.

Put a teaspoon of jam in each tartlet, then divide the chopped plum between them, followed by the crumble. Sprinkle each with chopped almonds.

Bake the tartlets in the preheated oven for 15–18 minutes, or until golden. Let cool for 5 minutes, then transfer to a wire rack. Eat warm or cold but not hot, as the jam will burn easily. Dust with confectioners' sugar, if you like.

coffee and pecan cupcakes with praline

These are best made and eaten on the same day, but the undecorated cakes will keep well in the freezer if you want to make a batch to decorate later. If time is really short, top them with a simple coffee-flavored water icing instead of the frosting and praline.

3 tablespoons instant coffee granules

6 tablespoons boiling water

1¼ cups sugar, plus 2 tablespoons

1½ sticks butter, softened and cubed

3 large eggs

1⅓ cups self-rising flour

⅔ cup chopped pecans

Frosting

1 cup confectioners' sugar

2 tablespoons heavy cream

10 tablespoons unsalted butter, softened

2 x 12-cup muffin pans, lined with 15 paper cupcake liners

a baking sheet, lined with baking parchment

Makes 15

Preheat the oven to 350°F.

Tip the coffee into a cup with the boiling water and the 2 tablespoons of the sugar. Stir together for a minute or so until the sugar has dissolved. Let cool.

Put the butter, ¾ cup of the sugar, and the eggs in the bowl of an electric mixer (or use a large mixing bowl and an electric whisk). Sift in the flour, drizzle in 3 tablespoons of the coffee syrup, and whisk together for a few minutes to combine. Stir half the pecans into the mixture; reserve the other half for the praline.

Spoon the batter into the cupcake liners. Bake in the preheated oven for 20 minutes, or until risen and lightly golden. Transfer the cupcakes to a wire rack. While they are still warm, make a few indentations with a fork in the top of each one and carefully drizzle over a little of the remaining coffee syrup, letting it seep into the cakes as you do so. Let cool completely.

Next, make the praline. Tip the remaining ½ cup sugar into a medium pan or skillet over low heat and heat gently. As soon as it has melted, increase the heat a little and let the sugar simmer and gradually turn to a deep golden caramel. Add the reserved pecans, give everything a quick stir, and tip the hot praline onto the prepared baking sheet. Spread it out slightly, then leave until cold and set.

To make the frosting, sift the confectioners' sugar into a bowl, add the cream and butter, and beat until smooth.

Spread the frosting onto the cold cupcakes with a round-bladed knife. Bash the praline with the end of a rolling pin to break it up, then crumble some on top of each cake.

spiced pumpkin cheesecakes with nutmeg icing

Have fun with these for Halloween—use themed cupcake cases and decorate with sugarcraft sprinkles.

Cheesecakes

5 tablespoons butter

4 oz. graham crackers, broken into pieces

6½ oz. cream cheese

½ cup cottage cheese

½ cup canned pumpkin purée

½ cup sugar

2 medium eggs, lightly beaten

2 pinches each of ground cloves, ginger, allspice, and nutmeg

orange sanding sugar, to decorate (optional)

Nutmeg icing

¼ cup sugar

3½ oz. cream cheese

½ teaspoon freshly grated nutmeg

a 12-cup muffin pan, lined with paper cupcake liners

Makes 12

Preheat the oven to 300°F.

First make the graham cracker crust for the cheesecakes. Melt the butter in a small pan and let cool slightly.

Grind the crackers to crumbs in a food processor. Add all but 1 tablespoon of the melted butter (reserve this for the icing) and whiz to combine. Divide between the cupcake liners and press down firmly with the back of a teaspoon.

Put the cheeses, pumpkin purée, sugar, beaten eggs, and spices in an electric mixer (or use a large mixing bowl and an electric whisk). Whisk until smooth and combined. Tip the mixture into a pitcher, then pour it into the cupcake liners, dividing it equally.

Bake the cakes in the preheated oven for 15 minutes. Let cool completely—they will set as they cool.

To make the nutmeg icing, whisk the ingredients together (including the reserved butter) and put a spoonful on each cheesecake. If you are not eating them immediately, refrigerate them but let them come to room temperature before eating. Sprinkle with sanding sugar, if you like. They are soft-set, so they are best eaten with teaspoons.

cookies

prune, cinnamon, and toasted walnut cookies with cinnamon icing

French prunes from Agen are a juicy and delicious addition to these chewy cookies, but raisins would also be a good choice. If you are making the cookies at Christmas or are feeling decadent, substitute half the water in the icing with brandy.

½ cup walnut pieces

6½ tablespoons butter, softened

¾ cup packed light brown sugar

1 large egg, lightly beaten

2 tablespoons cream cheese

⅔ cup white whole-wheat and ⅔ cup self-rising flour (or use all self-rising flour)

2 teaspoons ground cinnamon

a pinch of salt

1 cup pitted, soft Agen prunes, snipped into small pieces

Cinnamon icing

¼ cup confectioners' sugar

2 or 3 pinches of ground cinnamon

2 *baking sheets, oiled*

Makes about 20

Preheat the oven to 400°F.

Spread the walnuts on a baking sheet and toast in the preheated oven for 5 minutes, then let cool.

Put the butter and sugar in an electric mixer (or use a large mixing bowl and an electric whisk) and beat until light and fluffy. Add the egg and cream cheese and mix again to combine. Sift in the flours, the cinnamon, and salt and mix again. Fold in the toasted walnuts and the prunes with a large metal spoon.

Drop craggy mounds of the batter onto the prepared baking sheets—about 1 heaping dessertspoonful each. Leave room between them to allow the cookies to spread as they bake; 6 or 7 per baking sheet is about right, so you will need to cook them in batches. Bake the cookies in the preheated oven for 10–12 minutes, or until golden. Let cool for a few minutes, then transfer to a wire rack to cool completely.

To make the cinnamon icing, sift the confectioners' sugar and cinnamon into a small bowl. Add 2 teaspoons cold water and mix—you want a drizzling consistency, so add a few more drops of water if needed. Drizzle a little icing over each cookie and let set.

apricot, cherry, and pine nut oat cookies

These are speedy and ideal to make with kids, as the batter won't come to any harm if it is rolled and prodded by little fingers. For a more grown-up variation, omit the cherries and add a level teaspoon of chopped fennel seeds with the oats.

⅓ cup dried apricots

⅓ cup undyed glacé cherries

3 tablespoons pine nuts

6½ tablespoons butter, softened

¼ cup light muscovado or packed light brown sugar

½ cup all-purpose flour

⅔ cup old-fashioned rolled oats

2 baking sheets, oiled

Makes about 18

Preheat the oven to 375°F.

Chop the apricots and cherries into small pieces and roughly chop the pine nuts.

Put the butter, sugar, flour, and oats in an electric mixer (or use a large mixing bowl and an electric whisk) and beat until combined. Stir in the chopped apricots, cherries, and pine nuts.

Bring the cookie dough together with your hands. Break off walnut-sized pieces and roll them into balls.

Arrange the balls of dough on the prepared baking sheets and press each one to flatten it slightly. Bake the cookies in the preheated oven for 15–18 minutes, or until lightly golden. Transfer the cookies to a wire rack to cool.

mini peanut butter and maple refrigerator cookies

These small, chunky cookies are very simple to make. Once made and chilled, the dough will keep for a couple of weeks in the fridge, so you can bake the cookies as and when you need them. The dough also freezes well—defrost, then slice and bake.

1½ sticks butter, softened and cubed

¾ cup crunchy peanut butter

2 tablespoons maple syrup

¾ cup plus 2 tablespoons light muscovado or packed light brown sugar

2⅛ cups all-purpose flour, sifted

1 teaspoon baking powder

a pinch of salt

1 large egg, lightly beaten

demerara sugar, for sprinkling

2–3 baking sheets, oiled

Makes about 48

Put the butter, peanut butter, maple syrup, and muscovado sugar in an electric mixer (or use a large mixing bowl and an electric whisk) and beat until combined. Tip in the flour, baking powder, and salt and add the beaten egg. Beat to combine, then bring the dough together with your hands.

Tip the dough out onto a lightly floured surface and divide it into 4. Roll each quarter into a sausage shape about 6½ inches in length and 1¼ inches in diameter. Wrap each one in plastic wrap and refrigerate for 30 minutes. After that, when the cookie dough is firm, you can cut slices from it to bake as you wish.

To bake the cookies, preheat the oven to 400°F.

Slice ½-inch thick circles of dough from the rolls; you should get about 12 cookies from each one.

Arrange the cookies on the prepared baking sheets. Lightly press the back of a fork into the top of each cookie to make an indentation and sprinkle with demerara sugar. Bake in the preheated oven for 10–12 minutes, or until golden. Let cool on wire racks.

salted caramel malt cookies

If you don't have a cutter the right size to make these, cut around a glass, the lid of a small pot, or similar. They are also cute made as mini-cookies using a 1¼-inch cutter. The sea salt adds a special something to the caramel, making the cookies dangerously good.

1⅔ cups self-rising flour

½ cup malted milk powder

a tiny pinch of salt

10 tablespoons butter, softened and cubed

¼ cup sugar

1 medium egg, lightly beaten

Salted caramel

⅓ cup dark muscovado or packed dark brown sugar

3 tablespoons butter

¼ teaspoon crushed sea salt, e.g. fleur de sel

½ x 14-oz. can sweetened condensed milk

a plain 2-in. cookie cutter

2 baking sheets, oiled

Makes about 24

Sift the flour into the bowl of an electric mixer. Add the malt powder, salt, and butter. Mix together until the mixture resembles bread crumbs.

Add the sugar and the beaten egg. Mix until combined, then bring the dough together with your hands. Wrap in plastic wrap and refrigerate for 30 minutes.

Preheat the oven to 375°F.

Tip half the dough out onto a lightly floured work surface and roll out until it is ⅜ inch thick. Using the cutter, stamp out rounds, then gently re-form the dough and continue until you have used it all.

Arrange the cookies on the prepared baking sheets. Bake in the preheated oven for 10 minutes, or until golden. Let cool on wire racks.

Repeat with the other half of the dough.

To make the salted caramel, gently heat the sugar, butter, and sea salt in a pan until the sugar has dissolved, stirring now and then. Pour in the condensed milk and heat over low heat for 5–6 minutes, stirring all the time, until the mixture is amalgamated. Increase the heat, and as soon as the caramel starts to bubble, take the pan off the heat. Let cool until barely warm.

Top each cookie with a swirl of the caramel, then let cool completely and set.

giant double chocolate chip cookies

Chewy and soft, these are a favorite to eat while still warm. I like chopping my own chocolate rather than using chocolate chips and often add a handful of roughly chopped unsalted shelled peanuts or hazelnuts too. If you want to make regular-sized cookies, just halve the size of the balls of dough that you bake.

2 sticks butter, softened

½ cup light muscovado or packed light brown sugar

¾ cup demerara sugar

2 large eggs, lightly beaten

2¼ cups self-rising flour, sifted

½ teaspoon baking powder

a pinch of salt

4 oz. bittersweet chocolate (about 50% cocoa solids)

4 oz. milk chocolate

2 baking sheets, lined with baking parchment

Makes about 16

Preheat the oven to 350°F.

Put the butter and sugars in an electric mixer (or use a large mixing bowl and an electric whisk) and beat for 3–4 minutes, or until creamy and fluffy. Add the beaten eggs and mix again.

Add the flour, baking powder, and salt and mix. Chop both types of chocolate into small chunks, then, using a large metal spoon, stir the chunks into the mixture. Break off golf ball-sized pieces and roll them into balls.

Arrange the balls of dough on the prepared baking sheets. Leave room between them to allow the cookies to spread as they bake—they will end up being about 4½ inches in diameter when they are done. You will need to cook them in batches. Bake in the preheated oven for 10–12 minutes, or until golden at the edges. Let cool for a couple of minutes, then transfer to a wire rack.

st. clement's macarons

Macarons have made a comeback in recent years and are now sold in all sorts of pretty colors. This is a simple way of making them and you can buy very good lemon or orange curd, which is ideal for filling them.

⅔ cup ground almonds

¾ cup sugar

2 teaspoons all-purpose flour

2 large egg whites

grated peel of 1 unwaxed lemon

grated peel of ½ orange

Filling

3 tablespoons cream cheese

3 tablespoons jarred lemon or orange curd

grated peel of ½ orange

2 baking sheets, lined with baking parchment

Makes 12

Preheat the oven to 350°F.

Tip all the ingredients (other than those for the filling) into an electric mixer. Alternatively, put them in a large mixing bowl and use an electric whisk. Beat together until well combined.

Put 24 teaspoonfuls of the batter onto the prepared baking sheets, leaving room for them to spread slightly. Bake in the preheated oven for 15–17 minutes, or until set and tinged with gold at the edges. Let cool for a few minutes, then transfer to wire racks.

To make the filling, whisk the cream cheese and curd together until smooth. Stir in the orange peel and refrigerate until needed. Sandwich the macarons together with the filling.

bittersweet chocolate thins with white chocolate filling

These delicate but very chocolatey cookies have a thin layer of sweet filling. If you want to cheat, fill them with hazelnut chocolate spread instead.

1 stick butter, softened

¼ cup sugar

1 cup plus 2 tablespoons all-purpose flour, sifted

2 tablespoons cocoa powder, plus extra for dusting

2½ oz. bittersweet chocolate (about 50% cocoa solids), broken into pieces

1 tablespoon vegetable oil

White chocolate filling

2½ oz. white chocolate, broken into pieces

2 teaspoons honey

2 tablespoons heavy cream

2 baking sheets, lined with baking parchment

Makes 10

Put the butter and sugar in an electric mixer (or use a large mixing bowl and an electric whisk) and beat until light and fluffy. Tip in the flour and cocoa and mix to combine. If the mixture doesn't come together straightaway, work it briefly with a spatula, then mix again until it comes together in a ball. Wrap in plastic wrap and refrigerate for 30 minutes.

To make the white chocolate filling, put the chocolate pieces, honey, and cream in a small heatproof bowl set over a pan of barely simmering water. Stir until the chocolate has melted and the mixture is smooth. Take the bowl off the heat, let cool, then refrigerate.

Preheat the oven to 325°F.

Lightly dust a work surface with cocoa. Halve the chilled dough and roll one half out on the work surface until it is about ¼ inch thick. Cut out 10 rectangles, 3 x 1½ inches, re-rolling the dough as necessary. Arrange the cookies on one baking sheet. Repeat with the other half of the dough. Bake in the preheated oven for 10 minutes. Let cool for a few minutes, then transfer to wire racks.

Melt the bittersweet chocolate with the oil in the same way you melted the white chocolate above. Take the bowl off the heat and dip the opposite corners of half the cookies into it. Let set.

Bring the filling back to room temperature and give it a stir. Spread a layer of filling on the underside of each of the plain cookies and place a chocolate-dipped cookie on top.

passion-fruit sandwich cookies

These are dainty, melt-in-the-mouth cookies sandwiched together with a passion-fruit cream. Choose passion fruit that have wrinkled skins, as they will be the most fragrant and juicy.

4 sticks butter, softened

⅔ cup confectioners' sugar, sifted, plus extra for dusting

3⅓ cups all-purpose flour, sifted

¾ cup cornstarch, sifted

Passion-fruit cream

6 tablespoons mascarpone

½ cup confectioners' sugar, sifted

pulp of 2 passion fruit

a piping bag, fitted with a wide plain or star tip

3 baking sheets, lined with baking parchment

Makes 14

Preheat the oven to 350°F.

Put the butter and sugar in an electric mixer (or use a large mixing bowl and an electric whisk) and beat together until pale and creamy. Tip in the flour and cornstarch and whisk again to combine.

Fill the piping bag with the mixture and use to pipe 3½-inch lengths onto the prepared baking sheets. Leave room between them to allow the cookies to spread as they bake. Bake in the preheated oven for 15–18 minutes, or until lightly golden at the edges. Let cool on the baking sheets.

To make the passion-fruit cream, mix all the ingredients together and refrigerate until needed.

Sandwich the cookies together with the passion-fruit cream. Lightly dust the tops with confectioners' sugar.

bright-as-a-button cookies

These are fun to make and kids will enjoy the brightly colored icings. Experiment with different food colors or you can, of course, ice them all one color. Alternatively, leave them plain, if you prefer.

Put the butter and sugar in an electric mixer (or use a large mixing bowl and an electric whisk) and beat together until pale and fluffy. Add the beaten egg, flour, ground almonds, baking powder, and lemon juice and mix to combine.

Tip the dough onto a lightly floured work surface and bring it together in a ball. Press the ball into a disc, wrap in plastic wrap, and refrigerate for at least 30 minutes.

Preheat the oven to 400°F.

Halve the chilled dough and roll one half out on the lightly floured work surface until it is about ¼ inch thick. Cut out 5 x 4-inch circles, using an upturned tea cup or similar to cut around. Arrange the cookies on one of the prepared baking sheets. Using

the ½-inch cookie cutter (or the tip of a small sharp knife), stamp out 2 rounds from the middle of each cookie to make buttonholes.

Repeat with the other half of the dough. Bake in the preheated oven for 10 minutes. Transfer to wire racks to cool.

To decorate, sift the confectioners' sugar into a bowl and stir in 3–4 tablespoons cold water— add it little by little until you have a thick icing consistency; you may not need it all. Divide the icing between 3 bowls and add a touch of food color to each. Add it with the very tip of a small knife—you really don't need much. Mix well.

Spread icing on each of the buttons. Let set for about 30 minutes before threading ribbon through the buttonholes.

6½ tablespoons butter,
softened and cubed

½ cup sugar

1 large egg, lightly beaten

1⅓ cups all-purpose flour

⅔ cup ground almonds

1 teaspoon baking powder

4 teaspoons freshly
squeezed lemon juice

To decorate

2⅔ cups confectioners' sugar

food coloring pastes or
liquid colors—hot pink,
orange, yellow, and green
work well together

*2 large baking sheets, lined
with baking parchment*

*a ½-inch plain cookie cutter
(optional)*

3 yards thin–medium ribbon

Makes 10

spiced brown sugar and clementine stars

These crisp, spiced cookies are pretty baked as stars but you can experiment with other shapes—hearts are cute too. If you are making them to hang on a Christmas tree, as soon as they come out of the oven make holes at one end of each cookie using a skewer, to thread ribbon through later.

6½ tablespoons butter, softened and cubed

⅓ cup dark muscovado or packed dark brown sugar

1 teaspoon corn syrup

1 medium egg, lightly beaten

1⅔ cups all-purpose flour, sifted

1 teaspoon baking powder

grated peel of 1 clementine

2 teaspoons ground cinnamon

a generous pinch each of ground nutmeg, allspice, and cloves

To decorate

⅔ cup confectioners' sugar

6–7 teaspoons freshly squeezed lemon juice

edible silver balls

edible white glitter

star cookie cutters in various sizes

2 large baking sheets, lined with baking parchment

Makes about 30

Put the butter, sugar, and corn syrup in an electric mixer (or use a large mixing bowl and an electric whisk) and mix until combined. Add the beaten egg little by little, alternating with a spoonful of flour, and still mixing. Add the rest of the flour, the baking powder, clementine peel, and spices. Mix to combine.

Tip the dough onto a lightly floured work surface and bring it together in a ball. Press the ball into a disc, wrap in plastic wrap, and refrigerate for at least 30 minutes.

Preheat the oven to 400°F.

Halve the chilled dough and roll one half out on the lightly floured work surface until it is about ³⁄₁₆ inch thick. Cut out stars with the cookie cutters and arrange the cookies on one of the prepared baking sheets. Gently re-form and re-roll the dough, then keep stamping out stars.

Repeat with the other half of the dough. Bake in the preheated oven for 8–10 minutes for smaller stars (about 2½ inches) and 12–14 minutes for larger stars (about 3½ inches). When they are ready, the dough will have risen slightly and the edges will be tinged with brown. Transfer to wire racks to cool.

To decorate, sift the confectioners' sugar into a bowl and stir in the lemon juice—add it little by little until you have a drizzling consistency. Decorate each star with a little icing (you can pipe it if you are feeling fancy). Finish with edible silver balls and glitter.

gingerbread men

The gingerbread men are crisp when baked, so are pretty resilient for kids to ice them with tubes of ready-made icing, if that should appeal.

6½ tablespoons butter

¼ cup dark muscovado or packed dark brown sugar

1¾ cups all-purpose flour

¾ teaspoon baking soda

2 teaspoons ground ginger

1 teaspoon ground cinnamon

¼ cup corn syrup

1 tablespoon blackstrap molasses

small colored sugar-coated chocolate drops or halved currants, for decoration

a 3-inch (top to bottom) gingerbread man cutter

2 baking sheets, lightly buttered

Makes about 18

Heat the butter and sugar together in a small pan until melted, stirring every now and then. Remove the pan from the heat and let cool slightly.

Sift the flour, baking soda, and ground ginger and cinnamon into the bowl of an electric mixer (or use a large mixing bowl and an electric whisk) and pour the melted butter mixture into it. Add the corn syrup and molasses and mix to combine. Bring together into a ball, wrap in plastic wrap, and refrigerate for 30 minutes.

Preheat the oven to 375°F.

Halve the chilled dough and roll one half out on the lightly floured work surface until it is about ¼ inch thick. Cut out men with the cutter and arrange the cookies on one of the prepared baking sheets. Gently re-form and re-roll the dough, then keep stamping out gingerbread men. Make indentations for eyes and mouths and add sugar-coated chocolate drops or currants for buttons.

Repeat with the other half of the dough.

Bake the gingerbread men in the preheated oven for 8 minutes, or until they are set and slightly firmer to the touch. Transfer to wire racks to cool.

hazelnut cheesecake bars

These bars will keep in the refrigerator for a day or so. They are ideal for coffee time or they also double up well as a simple dessert with poached fruit alongside.

1½ cups shelled, blanched whole hazelnuts

5 tablespoons butter

6½ oz. gingersnaps, broken into pieces

confectioners' sugar, for dusting

Cheesecake topping

14 oz. cream cheese

¾ cup sugar

3 large eggs

1¼ cups sour cream

a 9 x 13-in. baking pan, oiled

Makes 14

Preheat the oven to 350°F.

Spread the hazelnuts on a baking sheet and toast in the preheated oven for 10–12 minutes, then let cool. Reduce the oven temperature to 325°F.

Melt the butter in a small pan and let cool slightly. Tip the gingersnaps into a food processor. Add half the cooled hazelnuts and whiz together until you have fine crumbs. Add the melted butter and briefly whiz again. Tip the mixture into the prepared baking pan and press down firmly with the back of a spoon to make an even layer. Put the pan on a baking sheet.

To make the cheesecake topping, put all the ingredients in an electric mixer (or use a large mixing bowl and an electric whisk) and whisk to combine. Carefully pour the mixture on top of the cookie crust in the pan—the mixture will come pretty near the top. Roughly chop the remaining hazelnuts and scatter over the cheesecake. Bake in the preheated oven for 45 minutes. Let cool completely.

Refrigerate for 30 minutes before cutting into 14 bars. The cheesecake will be soft-set. Dust with confectioners' sugar.

chocolate fudge raspberry shortbread bars

This is a sophisticated, bite-sized number; the tart fruitiness of the raspberries complements the bittersweet chocolate.

1 stick butter, softened

¼ cup sugar

1 cup plus 2 tablespoons all-purpose flour

Chocolate topping

1¾ cups heavy cream

2 tablespoons confectioners' sugar

14 oz. bittersweet chocolate (70% cocoa solids), broken into small pieces

1½ cups raspberries

an 8-in. square pan, oiled

Makes 21

Preheat the oven to 375°F.

Put the butter and sugar in an electric mixer and beat for 3–4 minutes, or until pale and creamy. Add the flour and mix again for a few minutes to combine—the dough probably won't come together in a ball, but if you work it briefly with a wooden spoon and then your hands, it will come together. Tip into the prepared pan and press down firmly with the back of a spoon to make an even layer. Prick the base a few times with a fork. Bake in the preheated oven for 20 minutes, or until lightly golden. Let cool.

To make the chocolate topping, bring the cream and confectioners' sugar slowly to a boil in a pan. Put the chocolate pieces in a heatproof bowl. As soon as the cream begins to bubble, remove from the heat and pour into the bowl with the chocolate. Gently whisk together until the chocolate has melted and the mixture is smooth.

Stir the raspberries into the chocolate mixture, then pour it over the cooled shortbread base. Let cool completely, then refrigerate for 3 hours, or until set. Cut into 21 bars with a sharp knife.

pecan cheesecake swirl brownies

These brownies are gorgeous to look at and won't disappoint any brownie lover. Don't overcook them, as you want them to have soft, moist centers.

⅔ cup pecan halves

3½ oz. bittersweet chocolate (70% cocoa solids), broken into pieces

6½ tablespoons butter, softened

1 cup light muscovado or packed light brown sugar

2 large eggs, lightly beaten

¾ cup all-purpose flour

Cheesecake swirl

1 large egg

5 oz. cream cheese

3 tablespoons sugar

1 tablespoon all-purpose flour

a 7-in. square pan, oiled and baselined with baking parchment

Makes 16

Preheat the oven to 350°F.

Spread the pecans on a baking sheet and toast in the preheated oven for 10 minutes, then let cool.

Melt the chocolate pieces in a small heatproof bowl set over a pan of barely simmering water. Remove the bowl from the heat and let cool a little.

Roughly chop the toasted pecans.

Put the butter and sugar in an electric mixer (or use a large mixing bowl and an electric whisk) and beat until combined. Gradually add the beaten eggs, still mixing. Sift in the flour and add the slightly cooled melted chocolate. Mix again until combined. Using a large metal spoon, fold in the chopped pecans.

To make the cheesecake swirl, whisk all the ingredients together in a bowl until combined.

Tip the chocolate batter into the prepared pan and spread it evenly with a spatula. Drop blobs of the cheesecake mixture on top and, using a skewer or the end of a teaspoon, briefly swirl the cheesecake mixture into the top of the chocolate layer.

Bake the brownies in the preheated oven for 25 minutes. Let cool completely before cutting into 16 squares.

spiced date, apple, and sticky oat slices

My mother used to make these for me when I was studying for exams, so we called them exam slices. I still love them.

1½ cups pitted, soft dates, chopped

2 tart apples, cored, peeled, and chopped

finely grated peel of 1 orange

freshly squeezed juice of 2 oranges

1 teaspoon freshly squeezed lemon juice

1 teaspoon apple pie spice

Sticky oat layer

⅔ cup old-fashioned rolled oats

½ cup sugar

¾ cup self-rising flour

3 tablespoons butter, softened and cubed

3 tablespoons corn syrup

1 large egg yolk

a 7-in. square pan, oiled

Makes 10

Tip the chopped dates, apples, orange peel and juice, lemon juice, and apple pie spice into a medium saucepan. Mix and heat over medium heat. Once everything has come to simmering point, reduce the heat to low and gently cook the fruit for 8–10 minutes, covered, until the apple has softened. Let cool.

Preheat the oven to 350°F.

To make the sticky oat layer, put all the ingredients in an electric mixer (or use a large mixing bowl and an electric whisk) and beat to combine. Tip half this mixture into the bottom of the prepared pan and press down firmly with the back of a spoon to make an even layer.

Spoon the cooled date and apple mixture on top of the oat base and top with the remaining oat mixture, pressing it down again to make an even layer. Bake in the preheated oven for 30 minutes. Let cool completely before cutting into 10 bars.

coconut, apricot, and lime slices

These are a modern version of the coconut slice. The traditional version has raspberry jam beneath the coconut topping, but I think these are all the better for their juicy apricot layer.

1 stick butter, softened

¼ cup demerara sugar

1 cup plus 2 tablespoons all-purpose flour

1 lb. dried apricots, chopped

grated peel and freshly squeezed juice of 3 limes

Coconut topping

2 large eggs

1 x 5½-oz. can coconut cream

¼ cup sugar

a scant cup desiccated coconut

a 9 x 13-in. baking pan, oiled

Makes 14

Preheat the oven to 350°F.

Put the butter and sugar in an electric mixer and beat for 3–4 minutes, or until pale and creamy. Add the flour and mix again for a few minutes to combine.

Tip the mixture into the prepared pan and press down firmly with the back of a spoon to make an even layer. Prick the base a few times with a fork. Bake in the preheated oven for 15–20 minutes, or until lightly golden. Leave the oven on.

Meanwhile, put the apricots and lime peel and juice in a medium pan with ¼ cup cold water and bring to simmering point. Gently cook, covered, for 8–10 minutes, or until soft and mushy. Add another tablespoon of water if the mixture seems too dry as it simmers. Let the apricots cool slightly, then transfer to a food processor and whiz to a thick purée.

To make the coconut topping, lightly beat the eggs in the electric mixer, then add the coconut cream, sugar, and desiccated coconut and mix to combine.

Spread the apricot purée on top of the baked base and top with the coconut mixture, spreading it evenly. Bake for 40–45 minutes, or until golden. Let cool completely before cutting into 14 slices.

cherry marzipan streusel squares

These are also a favorite when made with raspberry or plum jam.

¾ cup all-purpose flour

3 tablespoons butter, chilled and diced

1 tablespoon confectioners' sugar

5 tablespoons cherry jam

Streusel topping

⅔ cup all-purpose flour

⅛ cup sugar

2 tablespoons butter, softened and cubed

1¾ oz. marzipan, diced

⅓ cup undyed glacé cherries, chopped

½ cup slivered almonds

Almond layer

6½ tablespoons butter, softened and cubed

⅓ cup sugar

2 large eggs, lightly beaten

⅔ cup ground almonds

3 tablespoons all-purpose flour

a 7-in. square pan, oiled

Makes 12

For the pastry, put the flour, butter, and sugar in an electric mixer and whiz until the mixture resembles bread crumbs. Add 2 tablespoons cold water and whiz again. Add a few more drops of water, if needed, to bring together into a dough.

Tip the dough out on a lightly floured work surface and roll out until it is about ⅛ inch thick. Trim the edges with a sharp knife to make a 7½-inch square. Line the base of the pan with the dough—it will come slightly up the inside of the pan all the way round. Refrigerate for 30 minutes.

Preheat the oven to 400°F.

To make the streusel topping, tip the flour and sugar into the electric mixer (or use a mixing bowl and an electric whisk) and whiz together. Add the butter and whiz until the mixture is crumbly. Tip into a bowl, if necessary, and stir in the marzipan, glacé cherries, and almonds.

To make the almond layer, mix all the ingredients together in the electric mixer until amalgamated.

Spread the cherry jam on top of the chilled pastry base. Spoon blobs of the almond mixture on top of the jam and spread them out with a spatula. Scatter the streusel topping over the top. Put the pan on a baking sheet and bake in the preheated oven for 40 minutes, or until lightly golden. Cover with foil towards the end of cooking to prevent over-browning. Let cool in the pan before cutting into 12 squares.

throw-together muesli bars

These are a really quick assembly job and will keep in an airtight container for several days, and they freeze well too. Perfect for picnics, long walks, and lunchboxes.

6½ tablespoons butter

¼ cup corn syrup

⅓ cup sugar

1¾ cups jumbo rolled oats

1 cup dried apricots, chopped

¾ cup pitted, soft dates, chopped

¼ cup golden raisins

¼ cup chopped unsalted pistachios

3 tablespoons chopped brazil nuts

3 tablespoons sesame seeds

1 tablespoon freshly squeezed lemon juice

an 8-in. square pan, well oiled

Makes 8

Preheat the oven to 375°F.

Heat the butter and corn syrup together in a small saucepan until melted.

Meanwhile, combine all the other ingredients in a large mixing bowl. Add the warm butter mixture and stir thoroughly to combine.

Tip the mixture into the prepared pan and press down firmly with the back of a spoon to make an even layer. Bake in the preheated oven for 25 minutes, or until golden. Let cool for 15 minutes or so, then, using a sharp knife, cut into 8 bars. Let cool completely before lifting the bars out of the pan.

nectarine and blueberry bars with lavender sugar

These bars are packed full of juicy fruit. You can leave out the lavender if it isn't your thing and the nectarines can be swapped for peaches, a similar quantity of plums or apricots, or a pint of mixed berries. In any case, the bars are best made and eaten on the same day.

3 large eggs

1 cup sugar

1¼ cups self-rising flour, sifted

1 teaspoon baking powder

½ teaspoon pure vanilla extract

1½ sticks butter, softened and cubed

½ tablespoon dried lavender buds

3 ripe but firm nectarines

1½ cups blueberries

1 tablespoon cornmeal

Lavender sugar

½ tablespoon dried lavender buds

2 tablespoons sugar

grated peel of 1 unwaxed lemon

a 9 x 13-in. baking pan, lined with baking parchment and lightly buttered

Serves 14

Preheat the oven to 350°F.

Put the eggs, sugar, flour, baking powder, vanilla, butter, and lavender in an electric mixer (or use a large mixing bowl and an electric whisk) and whisk together. Pit the nectarines, chop them into bite-size pieces, and stir into the mixture along with the blueberries.

Dust the bottom of the prepared pan with the cornmeal and a very small amount of flour. Spoon the batter into the pan and spread it evenly with a spatula.

To make the lavender sugar, mix the ingredients together in a bowl, then scatter evenly over the batter.

Bake in the preheated oven for 35 minutes, or until risen and golden. Let cool in the pan before cutting into 14 bars.

sticky toffee bars with toffee fudge drizzle

Another day, try replacing the ginger with ⅓ cup golden raisins in the mix and use maple syrup in the icing instead of the ginger syrup. Both versions always seem to vanish very quickly.

1½ sticks butter, softened

½ cup dark muscovado or packed dark brown sugar

⅔ cup corn syrup

⅛ cup blackstrap molasses

1½ cups self-rising flour

1 teaspoon pure vanilla extract

3 large eggs

2 tablespoons heavy cream

2 balls stem ginger in syrup, drained and finely chopped

Toffee fudge icing

3 tablespoons butter

1 tablespoon of the syrup from the jar of stem ginger

2 tablespoons heavy cream

⅛ cup dark muscovado or packed dark brown sugar

⅓ cup confectioners' sugar

a 9 x 13-in. baking pan, lined with baking parchment and lightly buttered

Serves 14

Preheat the oven to 350°F.

Put the butter, sugar, corn syrup, molasses, flour, vanilla, eggs, and cream in an electric mixer (or use a large mixing bowl and an electric whisk) and beat until combined. Stir in the chopped stem ginger.

Tip the mixture into the prepared pan and spread it evenly with a spatula. Bake in the preheated oven for 25–30 minutes, or until risen and just set in the middle. Let cool completely in the pan.

To make the toffee fudge icing, put the butter, ginger syrup, cream, and muscovado sugar in a medium pan over low heat and leave until the butter has melted and the sugar dissolved. Remove the pan from the heat, sift in the confectioners' sugar, then whisk it in.

Remove the cake from the pan and drizzle the icing over it. Let set before cutting into 14 bars.

lemon squares

These look pretty as they are, lightly dusted with confectioners' sugar, but I sometimes top each square with a slice of fig or strawberry too.

¾ cup all-purpose flour

¼ cup confectioners' sugar, plus extra for dusting

5 tablespoons unsalted butter, chilled and cubed

1–2 figs, very thinly sliced, to decorate (optional)

Lemon layer

3 large eggs

1⅛ cups sugar

finely grated peel of 1 unwaxed lemon

⅔ cup freshly squeezed lemon juice (from 3–4 lemons)

⅓ cup all-purpose flour, sifted

a 7-in. square pan, oiled

Makes 16

Preheat the oven to 350°F.

First prepare the pan. Place 2 wide strips of baking parchment from one side to the other of the pan so that they form a cross on the bottom—this will help you to lift the cake out of the pan when it is cooked. Place a square of baking parchment on top of the strips, as you would usually do to line the bottom of a pan.

Put the flour, confectioners' sugar, and butter in an electric mixer (or use a large mixing bowl and an electric whisk) and whiz until the mixture resembles bread crumbs. Tip the mixture into the prepared pan and press down firmly with the back of a spoon to make an even layer. Prick the cookie crust a few times with a fork. Bake in the preheated oven for 12–15 minutes, or until lightly golden. Reduce the oven temperature to 300°F.

To make the lemon layer, put the eggs, sugar, and lemon peel in the electric mixer and beat for a minute or so. With the beaters still going, gradually pour in the lemon juice, then add the flour and mix to combine.

Spread the lemon mixture on top of the baked cookie crust. Bake for 45 minutes, by which time the lemon layer will be set and the top slightly crusty. Let cool completely.

Run a sharp knife around the edges, then lift out of the pan. Lightly dust with confectioners' sugar and cut into 16 squares. Decorate with the thin slices of fig, if using.

in a flash

lime drizzle cake with coconut frosting

If you want to make this look extra special, add a few shavings of toasted fresh coconut to the top.

1½ sticks butter, softened

¾ cup sugar

1⅛ cups self-rising flour, sifted

3 eggs

finely grated peel of 2 limes

Lime drizzle

½ cup confectioners' sugar

freshly squeezed juice of 2 limes

Coconut frosting

6 oz. cream cheese

5 tablespoons coconut cream

2 tablespoons confectioners' sugar

grated peel of 1 lime (use a zester, if you have one, rather than a fine grater)

a 7-in. round, deep cake pan, lightly buttered and baselined with baking parchment

Serves 8

Preheat the oven to 350°F.

Put the butter, sugar, flour, eggs, and lime peel in an electric mixer (or use a large mixing bowl and an electric whisk) and beat until combined.

Spoon the batter into the prepared pan and spread it evenly with a spatula. Bake in the preheated oven for 50–55 minutes, or until a skewer comes out clean when inserted into the center of the cake.

Meanwhile, to make the lime drizzle, sift the confectioners' sugar into a bowl and stir in the lime juice, then set aside.

To make the coconut frosting, whisk the cream cheese, coconut cream, and confectioners' sugar together in a bowl, then refrigerate until needed.

When the cake is ready, remove it from the oven and, using a small, fine skewer, make a few holes over the surface of the cake. Spoon over the lime drizzle. Let the cake cool completely in its pan.

Once cold, pop the cake out of the pan, remove the parchment paper, and spread the frosting over the top. Sprinkle with the lime peel.

simple fruitcake

This energy-giving cut-and-come-again cake is full of fruit and nuts and uses agave nectar—a low-GI, natural fructose sweetener—so a slice will keep hunger at bay. Agave nectar is now available in many supermarkets. If you want to make this cake more celebratory, brush warm, smooth apricot jam over it and decorate with small dried apricots and pecan halves.

⅔ cup dried apricots or figs

⅔ cup pitted, soft Agen prunes

1 cup shelled pecans, almonds, hazelnuts, or walnuts, or a mixture

10 tablespoons butter, softened

½ cup packed light brown sugar

1⅛ cups self-rising flour

1 teaspoon ground cinnamon

3 large eggs, lightly beaten

1 cup golden raisins

juice and peel of 1 orange

juice and peel of 1 unwaxed lemon

2 tablespoons agave nectar or honey

2 pure cane rough-cut sugar cubes, roughly crushed

a 7-in. square pan, lined with baking parchment and buttered

Serves 12

Preheat the oven to 300°F.

Using scissors, snip the dried apricots and the prunes into small pieces. Roughly chop the nuts.

Put the butter and sugar in an electric mixer (or use a large mixing bowl and an electric whisk) and beat until combined and fluffy.

Sift the flour and cinnamon into another bowl.

Add the flour mixture and beaten eggs alternately to the butter and sugar, whisking on a low setting all the time.

Using a large metal or wooden spoon, stir in the chopped fruit and nuts, the raisins, orange and lemon juices and peels, and the agave nectar. Mix well.

Tip the mixture into the prepared pan and spread it evenly with a spatula. Sprinkle the crushed sugar over the cake, then bake in the preheated oven for 1¼ hours. Let cool in the pan.

black currant, berry, and hazelnut crumble cake

This recipe also works well using damson plum jam. Either way, treat yourself to some chilled Greek yogurt on the side.

1 tablespoons butter, softened

¾ cup sugar

2 large eggs

1 cup self-rising flour

⅓ cup cornmeal

1 teaspoon baking powder

finely grated peel of 1 small unwaxed lemon

¼ cup Greek yogurt

¾ cup black currant jam

1¼ cups raspberries

Crumble topping

⅔ cup blanched hazelnuts

⅓ cup demerara sugar

5 tablespoons butter, chilled and cubed

¾ cup self-rising flour

a 9-in. springform pan, lightly buttered and baselined with baking parchment

Serves 12

Preheat the oven to 350°F.

To make the crumble topping, chop the nuts by hand or pulse them in a food processor—you want them to be roughly chopped. Mix the sugar, butter, and flour in an electric mixer until combined, then add 1 tablespoon cold water and briefly whiz again until the mixture resembles bread crumbs. Mix in the nuts. Alternatively, you can rub the butter into the flour by hand in a mixing bowl, then stir in the sugar, water, and nuts. Set aside.

Put the butter, sugar, eggs, flour, cornmeal, baking powder, lemon peel, and Greek yogurt in an electric mixer and mix until combined.

Spoon the mixture into the prepared pan and spread it evenly. Tip the jam into a bowl and mix it with a spoon to loosen it, then put spoonfuls over the top of the cake batter. Using the tip of a round-bladed knife, gently spread the jam by lightly swirling it into the top of the batter. Sprinkle a third of the crumble mixture on top, scatter the raspberries over this, then finish with the remaining crumble topping.

Put the pan on a baking sheet and bake in the preheated oven for 1 hour 5 minutes–1 hour 10 minutes, until just set in the middle. Let cool in the pan before releasing it, removing the base paper, and transferring to a plate or cutting board to slice.

mocha swirl bread with espresso icing

The fromage frais in this quick bread keeps the fat content down and the cornmeal gives it a lovely crunchy crust.

1 slightly rounded tablespoon espresso instant coffee powder

1 tablespoon boiling water

¾ cup fromage frais or farmer's cheese

½ cup cornmeal

1 stick butter, softened

1 cup sugar

3 large eggs

1⅝ cups self-rising flour

½ teaspoon baking soda

1 teaspoon pure vanilla extract

2 teaspoons cocoa powder

Espresso icing

⅔ cup confectioners' sugar

1 slightly rounded teaspoon espresso instant coffee powder

an 8½ x 4½ x 3-in. loaf pan, lightly buttered and baselined with baking parchment

Serves 8-10

Preheat the oven to 350°F.

Put the espresso powder and boiling water in a cup and stir to dissolve, then let cool.

Next, take a scant tablespoon from the fromage frais and set it aside for the icing. Put the remaining fromage frais with the cornmeal, butter, sugar, eggs, flour, and baking soda in an electric mixer (or use a large mixing bowl and an electric whisk) and beat until combined. Transfer half the mixture to another bowl. Stir the vanilla into the first bowl. Stir the dissolved coffee and the cocoa into the second bowl.

Spoon the 2 batters into the prepared loaf pan in 3 layers, alternating spoonfuls of each batter in each layer to resemble a chequerboard. Finally, using a skewer, gently swirl the layers together a few times until you have a definite swirl pattern on top of the loaf.

Bake in the preheated oven for 55 minutes, or until risen and the loaf is a lovely golden color on top. Let cool in the pan.

To make the espresso icing, sift the confectioners' sugar into a bowl and mix in the espresso powder along with the reserved tablespoon of fromage frais. Add enough cold water to make the icing a spreadable consistency—about 2 teaspoonfuls—but add it gradually, stirring, as you might not need it all.

Run a knife around the edges of the cold bread in the pan to release it. Turn it out, remove the parchment paper, and spread the icing on top. Let set before slicing.

crunchy prune and vanilla custard brioche cakes

These individual cakes have an indulgent fruity custard hiding under their crunchy topping. They are also good made with limoncello instead of the brandy, but leave out the alcohol altogether if you prefer. If time is really short, use muffin liners instead of making your own liners. These are best eaten on the day they are made.

2 large eggs

2 tablespoons Armagnac or other brandy

4 tablespoons demerara sugar

2 x 4-oz. vanilla pudding snack cups

5 tablespoons butter

6½ oz. brioche

⅔ cup pitted prunes, snipped into small pieces

a 6-cup muffin pan, each hole well buttered and lined with a 7-in. square of baking parchment

Makes 6

Preheat the oven to 350°F.

In a mixing bowl and using a balloon whisk, whisk together the eggs, Armagnac, 1 tablespoon of the sugar, and the pudding snacks.

Melt the butter in a small pan and pour into another, large mixing bowl.

Cut the brioche into ½-inch squares. Toss the squares in the melted butter with 2 tablespoons of the sugar, mixing well. Divide half the squares between the parchment-lined cups in the muffin pan, pressing them down firmly to make a base.

Divide the prune pieces between each muffin, then do the same with the egg mixture. Now add the rest of the brioche squares to the muffins, piling it up high. Scatter the remaining sugar over the top.

Bake in the preheated oven for 35 minutes, or until set and golden on top. Eat warm or cold.

no-bake chocolate, macadamia nut, and fig slices

These are as simple as can be and delicious with an espresso on the side. If you want to make them less sophisticated, for children, you can replace the macadamia nuts with any other type of nut and the dried figs with raisins or dried apricots.

6½ tablespoons unsalted butter

2 tablespoons honey

10 oz. bittersweet chocolate (50–70% cocoa solids), broken into pieces

3½ oz. milk chocolate, broken into pieces

6 graham crackers

⅔ cup shelled macadamia nuts

⅔ cup dried figs

cocoa powder, for dusting

a 7-in. square pan, oiled

Makes 16

Put the butter, honey, and both types of chocolate in a medium pan and melt gently, stirring from time to time.

Meanwhile, roughly chop the crackers, nuts, and figs. Stir into the melted chocolate mixture.

Tip the mixture into the prepared pan. Let cool completely before refrigerating for 2–3 hours to set. Cut into 16 slices.

peach, vanilla, and cherry shortcake

This is such a pretty option for a summer tea in the garden. Strawberries and raspberries also make a nice topping with a little shredded lemon verbena or, in the fall, thin slices of baked quince, a handful of blackberries, and a scattering of toasted nuts.

¾ cup all-purpose flour

5 tablespoons butter, softened and cubed

¼ cup confectioners' sugar, sifted

1 medium egg yolk

Topping

1 vanilla bean, split lengthwise

½ cup heavy or whipping cream, chilled

2 tablespoons confectioners' sugar, plus extra for dusting

2 ripe but firm peaches, pitted and sliced

1 cup cherries, pitted and halved

a squeeze of lemon juice

2 tablespoons shredded basil leaves

a baking sheet, lined with baking parchment

Serves 4

Put the flour, butter, sugar, and egg yolk in a food processor and mix together. If the dough doesn't come together, tip it into a bowl and work it with a spatula. Alternatively, you can make it by hand to start with. Tip the dough onto a lightly floured work surface and bring it together in a ball. Press the ball into a disc, wrap in plastic wrap, and refrigerate for 15 minutes.

Preheat the oven to 375°F.

Tip the dough out onto the lightly floured surface and roll or pat it out until it is big enough to cut out a 6-inch round—I use a plate or upturned bowl to cut around.

Transfer the round to the prepared baking sheet and bake in the preheated oven for 10–12 minutes, or until set and lightly golden at the edges. Let cool completely.

To make the topping, scrape the seeds out of the vanilla bean and into a bowl with the cream and half the confectioners' sugar. Whip into soft peaks.

Toss the peaches and cherries with the lemon juice, basil, and the remaining confectioners' sugar.

Dust the cold shortcake lightly with more confectioners' sugar, then top with the cream mixture and scatter the fruit mixture over the top. Serve immediately.

chocolate snaps with ricotta, pistachios, and candied fruit

These are easy but impressive and the flavors are similar to those of Sicilian *cannoli*. For a variation, try molding some of the baked rounds into tubes—use rounded teaspoonfuls of the mixture and bake in the same way. If you leave the rounds on the baking sheet to cool, as below, they are easy to remove and curl around the base of a wooden spoon or by hand. Bake just a few at a time and fill them with the same ricotta filling.

3 tablespoons butter

¼ cup demerara sugar

3 tablespoons corn syrup

¼ cup all-purpose flour

2 tablespoons cocoa powder, plus extra for dusting

a pinch of salt

Filling

1 cup ricotta, chilled

1 tablespoon confectioners' sugar

⅓ cup shelled, unsalted pistachios, finely chopped

2 oz. bittersweet chocolate (70% cocoa solids), finely chopped

⅓ cup chopped mixed candied peel

1 teaspoon orange flower water

a large baking sheet, lined with baking parchment

Makes 10

Heat the butter, sugar, and corn syrup together in a small pan until the butter has melted and the sugar dissolved, stirring every now and then. Pour into a mixing bowl. Sift in the flour, cocoa, and salt, mix thoroughly, and let cool for 15 minutes.

Preheat the oven to 325°F.

Drop 10 teaspoonfuls of the chocolate mixture onto the prepared baking sheet. Leave about 2½ inches between them to allow the snaps to spread as they bake. Flatten them very slightly with the back of the teaspoon before baking in the preheated oven for 8 minutes. Let cool on the baking sheet for 3–4 minutes before transferring to a wire rack to cool completely and become crisp—this will take only a matter of minutes.

Repeat with the second half of the mixture so that you end up with 20 rounds in total.

To make the filling, mix all the ingredients together in a bowl. Generously sandwich the snaps together with the filling. Lightly dust the top of each one with cocoa.

pear, mascarpone, and orange tarts

Using ready-made and ready-rolled puff pastry makes life easy here. Plum or apple slices would also work well as a topping for these tarts.

10 oz. puff pastry dough, thawed if frozen

3 tablespoons butter

½ cup mascarpone

3 tablespoons sugar, plus extra for sprinkling

finely grated peel of 1 small orange

½ cup ground almonds

1 large egg yolk

4 ripe but firm small pears, cored and thinly sliced (no need to peel)

3–4 tablespoons smooth apricot jam

¼ cup toasted slivered almonds

2–3 large baking sheets, lined with baking parchment and oiled

Makes 12

Preheat the oven to 425°F.

Take the pastry out of the refrigerator.

Melt the butter in a small pan and let cool slightly.

Put the mascarpone, sugar, orange peel, ground almonds, and egg yolk in a bowl and mix. Refrigerate until needed.

Halve the pastry and roll one half out on a lightly floured work surface until it is about 1/16 inch—any thicker than that and the pastry won't crisp up in the oven. Trim the edges with a sharp knife to make a 9 x 10-inch piece, then cut that into six 3 x 5-inch rectangles. Arrange the rectangles on one of the prepared baking sheets.

Repeat with the other half of the pastry.

Brush the edges of each rectangle with the melted butter and sprinkle a little sugar over them. Put 2 teaspoons of the mascarpone mixture in the center of each rectangle. Spread the mixture out using a small knife, leaving a border of about ⅜ inch all the way round.

Top each tart with overlapping slices of pear and scatter a little more sugar over the top. Bake the tarts in the preheated oven for 15 minutes, or until the pastry is golden and crisp. Transfer to a wire rack.

Warm the apricot jam in a small pan, then use to brush over the pear slices. Sprinkle the slivered almonds over the top, then let cool.

treats to keep

zucchini, carrot, and pear cake with poppy seed frosting

1½ cups all-purpose flour

¾ cup spelt flour

1 slightly rounded teaspoon baking powder

1 teaspoon baking soda

1 tablespoon ground cinnamon

2 pinches of ground cloves

4 large eggs

1⅓ cups light muscovado or packed light brown sugar

1 cup virgin coconut oil or canola oil

1 cup grated carrots (no need to peel)

⅔ cup grated zucchini (no need to peel)

2 medium pears, cored and chopped (no need to peel)

1 cup walnut or pecan pieces

⅔ cup golden raisins

Poppy seed frosting

5 tablespoons unsalted butter, very soft

6½ oz. chilled cream cheese

⅓ cup chilled Greek yogurt

1¼ cups confectioners' sugar, sifted

1 tablespoon poppy seeds

two 8-in. round cake pans, lightly buttered and baselined with baking parchment

Serves 12

Coconut oil often solidifies in its container, so immerse the pot or jar in a bowl of hot water, from the kettle, for about 10 minutes to melt the oil. If you want to make this cake completely dairy-free, replace the butter, cream cheese, and yogurt in the frosting with 6½ oz. soya cream cheese, sweetened with 2 tablespoons confectioners' sugar. This cake will store well for a few days, but even longer if kept in an airtight container in the refrigerator. Serve it at room temperature.

Preheat the oven to 350°F.

Sift the flours, baking powder, and baking soda into the bowl of an electric mixer (or use a large mixing bowl and an electric whisk). Tip any spelt left in the sieve into the bowl too. Add the cinnamon, cloves, eggs, sugar, and oil. Mix together.

In another bowl, mix the carrots, zucchini, pears, nuts, and raisins. Using a large metal spoon, fold these ingredients into the cake batter, making sure everything is thoroughly combined.

Spoon the batter into the prepared pans and spread it evenly with a spatula. Bake in the preheated oven for 40–45 minutes, or until risen, golden, and set in the center. Let cool in the pans.

To make the poppy seed frosting, whisk together the butter and cream cheese, add the yogurt and confectioners' sugar, and whisk again—an electric whisk makes quick work of this. Stir in the poppy seeds, then refrigerate until needed.

Tip the cold cakes out of the pans and peel off the parchment paper. Place one cake on a cutting board or serving plate, bottom-side up. Spread half the frosting over it. Put the other cake on top, top-side up, and spread the remaining frosting over the top.

tropical chai pineapple cake

¾ cup boiling water

3 chai tea bags

12 oz. trimmed fresh pineapple

8 oz. mixed soft dried tropical fruit, e.g. pineapple, papaya, mango, melon

3½ oz. pitted, soft dates

1 cup raisins

½ cup dark muscovado or packed dark brown sugar

1 teaspoon baking soda

1 tablespoon ground allspice

1 teaspoon freshly grated nutmeg

1 short cinnamon stick

3 star anise

¼ cup dark rum

10 tablespoons butter, chopped

grated peel of 2 limes

1 cup all-purpose flour

1 cup self-rising flour

⅔ cup shelled brazil nuts, chopped

2 large eggs, lightly beaten

3 tablespoons honey

dried pineapple slices, to decorate

an 8-in. springform cake pan, lightly buttered and baselined with baking parchment

Serves 16

This soft-textured, moist fruitcake keeps for up to two weeks and is flavored with chai tea, which has warm undertones of cinnamon and ginger. If you can't find soft dried tropical fruit, use dried apricots, pears, apples, peaches, or prunes, or a mixture, instead.

Pour the boiling water into a glass measuring cup, add the tea bags, stir, and set aside while you prepare the rest of the ingredients.

Chop the pineapple into small pieces and set aside.

Chop the dried fruit and the dates into small chunks. Put into a medium pan with the raisins, sugar, baking soda, all the spices, the rum, and butter. Discard the tea bags and pour the chai tea into the pan too. Stir together and bring the mixture to simmering point over gentle heat.

When the butter has melted, increase the heat and boil the mixture for 2 minutes exactly, then transfer the contents to a large mixing bowl. Stir in the pineapple and lime peel and let cool completely, giving it a stir from time to time, as and when you remember.

Preheat the oven to 325°F.

Remove the cinnamon stick and star anise from the mixture. Sift both flours into the bowl and add the chopped nuts and beaten eggs. Stir well.

Tip the batter into the prepared pan and spread it evenly with a spatula. Bake in the preheated oven for 1¾ hours, or until risen and deep golden. Let cool in the pan.

Remove the cake from the pan and peel off the parchment paper. Warm the honey in a small pan, then use to brush all over the cake. Decorate with dried pineapple slices.

banana and passion-fruit bread

For the best flavor, make sure your bananas are really ripe for this, even if they are at the stage when they have turned black in the fruit bowl and no one wants to eat them; they will be perfect to use in this bread.

1¾ cups self-rising flour

½ teaspoon baking soda

6½ tablespoons butter, softened and cubed

¾ cup sugar

2 large eggs, lightly beaten

3 passion fruit

3 very ripe bananas

To decorate

⅔ cup confectioners' sugar

1 passion fruit

dried banana slices, to decorate

an 8½ x 4½ x 3-in. loaf pan, lightly buttered and baselined with baking parchment

Serves 8-10

Preheat the oven to 350°F.

Sift the flour and baking soda into a bowl. Put the butter and sugar in an electric mixer (or use a large mixing bowl and an electric whisk) and beat until pale and fluffy. Add the beaten eggs and sifted flour mixture alternately to the bowl.

Halve the passion fruit and scoop out the pulp into a strainer set over a bowl. Using a teaspoon, press and stir the pulp to extract the juice. Discard the leftover seeds. Peel and mash the bananas. Add the passion-fruit pulp and mashed banana to the cake batter and mix again.

Tip the batter into the prepared loaf pan and spread it evenly with a spatula. Bake in the preheated oven for 55 minutes, or until golden and risen. Let cool in the pan.

To decorate, sift the confectioners' sugar into a small bowl. Halve the passion fruit and scoop out the pulp into the bowl—no need to strain the pulp this time. Mix together with a teaspoon. The confectioners' sugar will seem stiff at first, but persevere until is thoroughly mixed. If the glaze still seems a little thick, add a drop or two of cold water—the consistency of the glaze will depend on the size of the passion fruit and how ripe it is. You want the glaze to be a thick, spreadable consistency.

Tip the cold bread out of the pan and peel off the parchment paper. Spoon the glaze over the top of the bread and decorate with dried banana slices. Let set for about 30 minutes before slicing.

molasses, marmalade, and ginger loaf

This loaf keeps really well in a cookie tin or airtight container for several days. It freezes well too, but add the marmalade topping after defrosting. This is a good one to slice and take on picnics or wintry walks.

1 stick butter, softened and cubed

½ cup dark muscovado or packed dark brown sugar

1⅖ cups all-purpose flour, sifted

2 teaspoons baking powder

1 teaspoon ground ginger

2 large eggs, lightly beaten with ⅖ cup milk

¼ cup blackstrap molasses

5 tablespoons orange marmalade

3 balls stem ginger in syrup, drained and finely chopped

⅖ cup dried apricots, snipped into small pieces

an 8½ x 4½ x 3-in. loaf pan, lightly buttered and baselined with baking parchment

Serves 8-10

Preheat the oven to 375°F.

Put the butter and sugar in an electric mixer (or use a large mixing bowl and an electric whisk) and beat until combined. Tip in the flour, baking powder, and ground ginger and add the egg mixture and molasses. Mix everything together. Stir in 3 tablespoons of the marmalade, the chopped ginger, and the apricots.

Tip the batter into the prepared pan and bake in the preheated oven for 50 minutes. Let cool in the pan. Towards the end of cooling, gently heat the remaining marmalade and spread it over the top of the bread. Let cool completely before carefully tipping the bread out of the pan and peeling off the parchment paper.

apple and amaretto cake

This cake is quick to make and can be left to bake while you get on with other things. It freezes well and is delicious as is; for added indulgence, whipped cream mixed with a little confectioners' sugar and almond-flavored Amaretto makes a heavenly accompaniment.

2 Honeycrisp or Macoun apples

2⅔ cups all-purpose flour, sifted

1 tablespoon baking powder

2 teaspoons ground cinnamon

14 tablespoons butter, softened and cubed

¾ cup light muscovado or packed light brown sugar

2 large eggs

⅓ cup milk

⅓ cup Amaretto

1⅓ cups golden raisins

To decorate

3 small, red apples

2 tablespoons honey

a 9-in. springform pan, lightly buttered and baselined with baking parchment

Serves 8-10

Preheat the oven to 350°F.

Core, peel, and chop the apples into ½-inch chunks.

Tip the flour, baking powder, cinnamon, butter, sugar, eggs, milk, and Amaretto into the bowl of an electric mixer (or use a large mixing bowl and an electric whisk) and beat together until combined.

Using a large metal spoon, thoroughly stir in the chopped apples and the raisins.

Spoon the batter into the prepared pan and spread it evenly with a spatula.

To decorate, quarter the 3 red apples. Don't peel them, but core them and thinly slice the quarters. Arrange the slices, slightly overlapping, on top of the cake in concentric circles.

Put the pan on a baking sheet and bake in the preheated oven for 1½–1¾ hours, or until risen and golden and the apple slices on top are burnished. Cover the cake with foil towards the end of cooking to prevent over-browning, if necessary.

Warm the honey in a small pan, then use to brush over the top of the cake. Let cool in the pan before releasing it, peeling off the parchment paper, and transferring to a plate or cutting board to slice.

after-school stop-light jam tarts

A goodie to have in the house for children when they come home from school, starving.

10 oz. ready-made pie dough

⅛–⅓ cup each raspberry, apricot, and greengage jam

a little beaten egg, for brushing (optional)

a plain or fluted 3½-in. cookie cutter

a 12-cup shallow bun pan, oiled

Makes 12

On a lightly floured work surface, roll out the pastry until it is about ⅛ inch thick. It may be easier to roll out half at a time. Using the cutter, stamp out 12 rounds and use to line the cups of the bun pan. Reserve the pastry trimmings. Chill the pastry-lined pan for 30 minutes.

Preheat the oven to 400°F.

Put about 2 teaspoonfuls of raspberry jam in 4 of the tarts, apricot jam in another 4, and greengage jam in the rest. Don't overfill them, otherwise the jam will bubble over the sides while they are cooking.

Re-roll the pastry trimmings and cut out short, thin strips of pastry. Place 2 parallel strips on top of each tart, twisting the strips as you do so and trimming them to fit the tarts. Press down the ends. Now place 2 more parallel strips at right angles to the first pair to create a lattice effect. Brush the lattice with a little beaten egg, if you like—it helps the pastry to brown.

Bake in the preheated oven for 20 minutes. Let cool for 5 minutes, then transfer to a rack to cool completely.

honey, toasted pine nut, and pumpkin-seed bars with chocolate topping

Vary the dried fruit you use in these chewy, fruity bars according to what you have handy. They are a hit with children and adults alike.

3 tablespoons pine nuts

2 tablespoons pumpkin seeds

1½ sticks butter

½ cup packed light brown sugar

3 tablespoons honey

⅔ cup dried sour cherries or cranberries, or chopped dried apricots, pears, peaches, or prunes, or a mixture

2 cups old-fashioned rolled oats

a pinch of salt

6½ oz. milk chocolate, broken into pieces

an 8-in. square pan, lightly buttered

Makes 24

Preheat the oven to 350°F.

Spread the pine nuts and pumpkin seeds on a baking sheet and toast in the preheated oven for 5 minutes, or until lightly golden. Let cool, then roughly chop.

Gently heat the butter, sugar, and honey together in a small pan until melted, stirring every now and then. Remove the pan from the heat and let cool slightly.

Tip the dried fruit and oats into a large mixing bowl. Add the salt and the chopped pine nuts and seeds. Pour in the warm butter mixture and mix well.

Tip the batter into the prepared pan and press down firmly with the back of a spoon to make an even layer. Put the pan on a baking sheet. Bake in the preheated oven for 30 minutes, or until lightly golden.

Meanwhile, melt the chocolate in a heatproof bowl set over a pan of barely simmering water. Pour into the pan, then let cool completely.

Remove from the pan and cut into 24 bars.

really lemony gluten-free cake

The lemon peel and juice make this cake lovely and moist, and it will keep in an airtight container for several days—store it whole and cut it as needed.

14 tablespoons butter, softened

1 cup sugar

4 large eggs

1 cup plus 2 tablespoons gluten-free self-rising white flour blend, sifted

2 teaspoons gluten-free baking powder

⅓ cup cornmeal

finely grated peel and juice of 1 lemon

Lemon syrup

½ cup confectioners' sugar

finely grated peel and freshly squeezed juice of 3 lemons

Candied lemons

1¼ cups sugar

2 lemons

an 8-in. square pan, lightly buttered and baselined with baking parchment

Serves 16

Preheat the oven to 350°F.

Put the butter, sugar, eggs, flour, baking powder, cornmeal, and lemon peel and juice in an electric mixer (or use a large mixing bowl and an electric whisk) and beat until combined. Spoon the mixture into the prepared pan. Bake in the preheated oven for 45 minutes, or until risen, firm to the touch, and golden.

Meanwhile, to make the lemon syrup, sift the confectioners' sugar into a bowl and whisk in the lemon peel and juice with a balloon whisk. Set aside to let the sugar dissolve.

To make the candied lemons, put the sugar and 1 cup water into a pan. Gently heat, stirring, until the sugar has dissolved. Slice the lemons and flick out as many of the pips as you can. Add the lemon slices to the liquid in the pan—you want the lemons to cook more or less in a single layer. Bring to a simmer, then gently cook, uncovered, for 45 minutes, stirring from time to time.

When the cake is ready, take it out of the oven and make holes all over the surface with a fork. Spoon the lemon syrup over the cake, allowing it to seep in between spoonfuls—it will seem like a lot, but gluten-free flour is very absorbent. Let the cake and candied lemons cool completely.

Turn the cake out of the pan and arrange the candied lemons on top, discarding the liquid they were cooked in.

hazelnut, orange, and marsala raisin biscotti

Biscotti are crunchy Italian double-baked cookies and they will keep for a month or so, making them a great standby. Dip the biscotti into Vin Santo, limoncello, tea, or a good espresso, as you eat them.

⅔ cup raisins

2 tablespoons Marsala

2 cups self-rising flour

3 tablespoons cocoa powder

1 teaspoon baking powder

¾ cup sugar

2 large eggs, lightly beaten

finely grated peel of
1 large orange

⅔ cup blanched hazelnuts,
roughly chopped

*2 baking sheets, lined with
baking parchment*

Makes about 30

Preheat the oven to 350°F.

Put the raisins in a small bowl with the Marsala, stir, and let soak for at least 15 minutes.

Tip the flour, cocoa, baking powder, and sugar into a food processor and whiz to mix. Add the beaten eggs and orange peel and whiz again for a couple of minutes until the mixture resembles coarse bread crumbs. Tip the mixture into a mixing bowl and add the raisins and their liquid, and the chopped hazelnuts.

Using a spatula or wooden spoon, mix and knead everything together in the bowl until it starts to clump together—this will take a few minutes. Tip the dough out onto a lightly floured work surface and bring together into a ball with your hands.

Halve the dough and briefly knead each half. Roll each one into an 8-inch long log. Put both logs onto one of the prepared baking sheets, leaving about 4 inches between them to allow them to spread as they bake. Bake in the preheated oven for 35 minutes.

Remove the baked logs from the oven and let cool for 15 minutes, or until they are cool enough to handle. Meanwhile, reduce the oven temperature to 300°F.

Using a serrated bread knife, slice the logs on the diagonal into ⅜-inch thick slices. You should get about 15 slices from each log. Discard the ends.

Arrange the slices on the 2 baking sheets in a single layer and bake them for a further 20 minutes to dry them out. Let cool on wire racks.

special
occasions

mulled wine and cranberry tea bread

This bread is studded with juicy fruit and nuts, perfect for fall and winter. It is delicious sliced and eaten as it is or spread with unsalted butter.

a wine-mulling spice bag

¾ cup light, fruity red wine

1 tablespoon honey

½ cup dried figs

⅓ cup crystallized stem ginger

½ cup whole blanched almonds

⅓ cup each dried cranberries and dried sour cherries (or use ⅔ cup golden raisins)

½ cup light muscovado or packed light brown sugar

2 large eggs, lightly beaten

grated peel of 2 oranges

1 cup fresh cranberries

1¾ cups self-rising flour

1 teaspoon ground cinnamon

½ teaspoon ground allspice

Topping

½ cup dried cranberries (or dried sour cherries, or golden raisins)

2 tablespoons orange juice

¼ cup red currant jelly

an 8½ x 4½ x 3-in. loaf pan, lightly buttered and baselined with baking parchment

Serves 12

First make the mulled wine. Put the wine-mulling spice bag in a medium pan with the red wine and honey. Slowly bring to a simmer, stirring now and then. Leave over very low heat for 5 minutes, then take the pan off the heat and set aside.

Roughly chop the figs, ginger, and almonds and mix with the dried cranberries and cherries and the sugar in a mixing bowl. Remove the spice bag from the mulled wine, then pour the warm wine over the dried fruit and let soak for 30 minutes.

Preheat the oven to 325°F.

Stir the beaten eggs, orange peel, and the fresh cranberries into the soaked dried fruit. Next, sift in the flour, cinnamon, and allspice. Mix together until thoroughly combined.

Spoon the batter into the prepared loaf pan. Bake in the preheated oven for 55 minutes, by which time the bread will have risen and slightly shrunk from the sides of the pan. Let cool in the pan, then run a table knife around the edge of the pan, tip the bread out, and peel off the parchment paper.

To make the topping, gently heat the cranberries, orange juice, and red currant jelly in a small pan over low heat, stirring until the jelly has dissolved.

Brush the top of the bread with some of the sticky juices from the topping, then spoon the cranberries along the center of the bread. Let cool before serving.

snowman cookies

These are fun to make with children. If you don't want to have to buy fondant icing in different colors, use red for both the noses and the mouths—or tiny pieces of candied peel also make fine snowman noses.

1¾ cups self-rising flour, sifted

6½ tablespoons butter, softened

½ cup packed light brown sugar

1 large egg

1 tablespoon corn syrup

a pinch of ground cinnamon (optional)

To decorate

confectioners' sugar, for dusting

14 oz. ready-to-roll white fondant icing

2 teaspoons corn syrup

24 currants, halved

about 2 oz. ready-to-roll orange fondant icing

about 2 oz. ready-to-roll red fondant icing

6 oz. ready-to-roll black, blue, or green fondant icing

a plain 3-in. cookie cutter

2 baking sheets, oiled

Makes 24

Put the flour, butter, sugar, egg, corn syrup, and cinnamon, if using, in the bowl of an electric mixer and beat together until combined. Bring the dough together with your hands, then wrap in plastic wrap and refrigerate for 1 hour or longer—even overnight is fine, if you want to get ahead.

Preheat the oven to 350°F.

Tip half the dough out onto a lightly floured work surface and roll out until it is ³⁄₁₆ inch thick. Using the cutter, stamp out 12 rounds and arrange them on the baking sheets. Bake in the preheated oven for 10–12 minutes, or until lightly golden. Let cool on wire racks.

Repeat with the other half of the dough.

To decorate, lightly dust the work surface and a rolling pin with confectioners' sugar. Roll out half the white icing until it is ⅛ inch thick. Using the cutter again, stamp out 12 rounds. Repeat with the other half of the icing.

Put a dab of corn syrup in the center of each cookie to act as glue and place a round of white icing on each one. Make 2 eyes on each snowman by pressing 2 currant halves into the icing quite firmly.

Next, using your hands, roll 24 small, carrot-shaped noses from the orange icing, making indentations along the length of each one with a small knife. Stick the noses onto the snowman faces with the tiniest dab of water.

Roll the red icing into 24 short, thin strips and pinch the ends. Stick one to each face for a mouth.

Using a rolling pin again, roll out the black, blue, or green icing, in batches, and cut out hat shapes. Make indentations for the brims. Stick the hats on, then let the snowmen dry for an hour or so before serving.

ultimate chocolate fudge cake with sponge candy

This cake has a light, not-too-rich crumb and is perfect for a birthday cake—just add candles. If you want to get ahead, you can freeze the filled and topped cake, then defrost and sprinkle with the sponge candy to serve.

2 tablespoons cocoa powder

3 tablespoons boiling water

1¾ cups self-rising flour

2 teaspoons baking powder

14 tablespoons butter, softened

1¼ cups light muscovado or packed light brown sugar

2 tablespoons heavy cream

1 teaspoon pure vanilla extract

4 large eggs, lightly beaten

Sponge candy

⅓ cup sugar

2 tablespoons corn syrup

1 tablespoon baking soda

Chocolate fudge frosting

6½ oz. bittersweet chocolate (about 50% cocoa solids), broken into pieces

⅔ cup heavy cream

1 tablespoon vegetable oil

two 8-in. cake pans, lightly buttered and baselined with baking parchment

a baking sheet, lined with baking parchment

Serves 8

Preheat the oven to 350°F.

Dissolve the cocoa in the boiling water, then let cool. Sift the flour and baking powder into a bowl.

Put the butter and sugar in an electric mixer (or use a large mixing bowl and an electric whisk) and beat for 3–4 minutes, or until smooth and fluffy. Mix in the cream, vanilla, and the cooled, dissolved cocoa. With the mixer running on a slow speed, add the beaten eggs and sifted flour mixture alternately to the bowl.

Spoon the batter into the prepared pans and spread it evenly with a spatula. Bake in the preheated oven for 25–30 minutes, or until firm to the touch. Let cool in the pans for 30 minutes. Tip out onto a wire rack and peel off the parchment paper. Let cool completely.

To make the sponge candy, put the sugar and corn syrup in a medium pan over gentle heat. Heat, stirring, until the sugar has melted. Increase the heat and bubble for 1 minute exactly. Take the pan off the heat and quickly stir in the baking soda—the mixture will turn white and frothy. Immediately pour it onto the prepared baking sheet and let cool until set.

To make the chocolate fudge frosting, put all the ingredients in a heatproof bowl over a pan of barely simmering water and leave until smooth and glossy, stirring now and then. Take the bowl off the pan and set aside to cool.

To assemble, place one cake on a cutting board or large serving plate and spread about a third of the chocolate fudge frosting over the top. Place the other cake on top and coat entirely in the rest of the frosting. Chop the sponge candy into small chunks and sprinkle on top of the cake—any leftovers are a cook's perk!

rosewater, pistachio, and grapefruit cake

You can buy crystallized pink rose petals in jars, or, to make your own, dip unsprayed petals in lightly beaten egg white followed by granulated sugar. Shake off the excess sugar, then let the petals dry on baking parchment until crisp. Serve the cake with Greek yogurt sweetened with a little honey.

1⅓ cups shelled, unsalted pistachios

1⅝ cups self-rising flour

1 tablespoon baking soda

10 tablespoons butter, softened and cubed

¾ cup sugar

3 large eggs, lightly beaten

2 tablespoons rosewater

¼ cup buttermilk

grated peel of 2 pink or red grapefruit

a few crystallized rose petals, to decorate

Grapefruit syrup

1 pink or red grapefruit

1 tablespoon rosewater

⅓ cup sugar

a 9-in. springform pan, lightly buttered

Serves 10-12

Preheat the oven to 350°F.

Begin by whizzing 1 cup of the pistachios in a food processor until finely ground. Roughly chop the remaining ⅓ cup and mix three-quarters of them with the ground pistachios. Reserve the rest for scattering on the cake to decorate.

Sift the flour and baking soda into the bowl of an electric mixer. Add the butter and mix together, on the lowest speed, until the mixture resembles clumpy bread crumbs. Add the pistachios, sugar, beaten eggs, rosewater, buttermilk, and grapefruit peel and mix until combined. The batter will be thick, so you will probably need to stop a couple of times to scrape the mixture off the beaters.

Tip the mixture into prepared pan and spread it evenly with a spatula. Bake in the preheated oven for about 45 minutes, or until golden and risen.

Towards the end of the cooking time, make the grapefruit syrup. Squeeze the juice of the grapefruit through a strainer and into a medium pan. Add the rosewater and sugar to the pan and gently heat together, stirring, until the sugar has dissolved. Increase the heat and boil for 2 minutes to make the liquid slightly more syrupy.

When the cake is ready, remove it from the oven and, using a small, fine skewer, make a few holes over the surface of the cake. Spoon over the warm grapefruit syrup, allowing it to seep in between spoonfuls. Let the cake cool completely in its pan.

Once cold, pop the cake out of the pan and scatter the reserved chopped pistachios and a few crystallized rose petals on top.

victoria sandwich with fresh mint and strawberries

The cake layers for this classic English cake are best eaten as fresh as possible. They are also delicious sandwiched together with good-quality raspberry jam or a citrus curd and some whipped cream.

14 tablespoons unsalted butter, softened

1 cup sugar

4 large eggs, lightly beaten

1 teaspoon pure vanilla extract

1⅔ cups self-rising flour, sifted

2 teaspoons baking powder

a pinch of salt

confectioners' sugar, for dusting

Filling

1 pint ripe strawberries

2 tablespoons confectioners' sugar

grated peel of 1 unwaxed lemon

⅔ cup crème fraîche or heavy cream, chilled

⅓ cup mascarpone, chilled

1 tablespoon shredded mint leaves

two 8-in. round cake pans, lightly buttered and baselined with baking parchment

Serves 8

Preheat the oven to 350°F.

Put the butter and sugar in an electric mixer (or use a large mixing bowl and an electric whisk) and beat for 3–4 minutes, or until pale and fluffy. Gradually add the beaten eggs with the beaters still running, followed by the vanilla, flour, baking powder, and salt. Mix until all the ingredients are combined.

Spoon the batter into the prepared pans and spread it evenly with a spatula. Bake in the preheated oven for 25 minutes, or until lightly golden and risen. Let cool in the pans for 30 minutes. Tip the cake layers out onto a wire rack and peel off the parchment paper. Let cool completely.

To make the filling, hull and thinly slice the strawberries, then mix in a bowl with half the confectioners' sugar and all the lemon peel. Let macerate for up to 30 minutes.

In another bowl, use a balloon whisk to whisk the crème fraîche and mascarpone together until smooth. Stir in the rest of the confectioners' sugar and the shredded mint.

To assemble, place one cake layer on a cutting board or large serving plate and spread the creamy filling over the top. Scatter the strawberries over the filling. Place the other cake on top and dust with confectioners' sugar.

white chocolate and apricot roulade

This summer stunner, once assembled, will hold for a couple of hours before serving —keep it in a cool place, but not the refrigerator. To make it look extra special, use a vegetable peeler to make curls from a block of white chocolate to scatter on top.

4 large eggs

½ cup sugar

2 pinches of saffron threads

¾ cup self-rising flour, sifted

3 tablespoons slivered almonds

1 tablespoon confectioners' sugar, plus extra for dusting

Apricot filling

seeds from 4 cardamom pods, crushed

1 tablespoon honey, preferably orange blossom

1 tablespoon freshly squeezed lemon juice

8 apricots, pitted and finely chopped

White chocolate cream

2½ oz. white chocolate, broken into pieces, plus extra if making curls

⅔ cup crème fraîche

¾ cup heavy cream

a 9 x 14-in. jelly roll pan, oiled and baselined with baking parchment

Serves 10-12

Preheat the oven to 375°F.

Break the eggs into a large heatproof mixing bowl and add the sugar and saffron. Place over a pan of simmering water, making sure the base doesn't touch the water. Using an electric whisk, whisk the ingredients for 5 minutes, or until pale and voluminous. Take the bowl off the heat. Using a large metal spoon, carefully fold the flour into the mixture.

Tip the mixture into the prepared pan and gently spread it evenly with a spatula. Sprinkle the slivered almonds over the top. Bake in the preheated oven for 12–15 minutes, or until lightly golden. Meanwhile, cover a large board with a sheet of baking parchment and sift the tablespoon of confectioners' sugar evenly over it.

When the cake is ready, let it set, out of the oven, for 10 minutes. Run a small, sharp knife around the edges before turning it upside down over the sugared parchment. Remove the pan and peel off the parchment paper. Roll up the cake from one of the shorter ends, rolling the sugared parchment with it as you do so—you may need to make a cut along the width of the cake about an inch in, to help you start rolling. Let cool completely.

To make the apricot filling, put all the ingredients in a pan and simmer gently, uncovered, for 10 minutes—you want the apricots to be soft, but still retaining their shape. Let cool, then refrigerate until needed.

To make the white chocolate cream, put the chocolate and 2 tablespoons of the crème fraîche in a small heatproof bowl over a pan of barely simmering water. Leave until melted, stirring from time to time. Take the bowl off the heat and let cool slightly. Whisk the cream in a bowl until it forms soft peaks, then stir in the remaining crème fraîche and the cooled chocolate mixture.

Unroll the cake onto a large board. Spread the white chocolate cream over it and scatter the apricot mixture on top. Roll up the roulade and dust with confectioners' sugar.

cinnamon blueberry cake

Make this cake on the day you are going to eat it, but let it cool completely before assembling and serving.

1½ sticks unsalted butter, softened

¾ cup sugar

4 large eggs, lightly beaten

a pinch of ground cinnamon

1⅓ cups self-rising flour, sifted

2 teaspoons baking powder

a pinch of salt

1 pint blueberries

Cinnamon frosting

6½ oz. chilled cream cheese

a scant ½ cup chilled crème fraîche or heavy cream

3 tablespoons unsalted butter, softened and cubed

1 cup confectioners' sugar, sifted, plus a little extra for dusting

2 teaspoons ground cinnamon

two 8-in. round cake pans, lightly buttered and baselined with baking parchment

Serves 8

Preheat the oven to 350°F.

Put the butter and sugar in an electric mixer (or use a large mixing bowl and an electric whisk) and beat for 3–4 minutes, or until pale and fluffy. Gradually add the beaten eggs with the beaters still running, followed by the cinnamon, flour, baking powder, and salt. Mix until all the ingredients are combined.

Spoon the batter into the prepared pans and spread it evenly with a spatula. Bake in the preheated oven for 20–25 minutes, or until lightly golden and risen. Let cool in the pans for 30 minutes. Tip the cake layers out onto a wire rack and peel off the parchment papers. Let cool completely.

To make the cinnamon frosting, whisk all the ingredients together to combine.

To assemble, place one cake on a cake stand or large serving plate and spread two-thirds of the cinnamon frosting over the top—a spatula or table knife is the ideal tool to use here. Scatter three-quarters of the blueberries on top of the frosting.

Place the other cake on the blueberries and spread the remaining frosting over the top. Finish with the rest of the blueberries. Dust with a little confectioners' sugar.

chocolate chestnut brownie torte

This torte has the texture of a brownie, but it is as light as a feather. It doesn't contain any flour, which is an added bonus for anyone with an intolerance to wheat. In addition to being dusted with cocoa, it also looks pretty scattered with chopped *marrons glacés*—candied chestnuts.

6½ oz. bittersweet chocolate (70% cocoa solids), broken into pieces

1½ sticks unsalted butter, cubed

5 large eggs, separated

¾ cup sugar

a pinch of salt

3½ oz. canned unsweetened chestnut purée

cocoa powder, for dusting

a few chopped, toasted hazelnuts, to decorate

a 9-in. springform pan, oiled and baselined with baking parchment

Serves 8

Preheat the oven to 350°F.

Put the chocolate and butter in a heatproof bowl set over a pan of barely simmering water. Stir until the chocolate has melted and the mixture is smooth and glossy. Take the bowl off the heat and let cool slightly.

Put the egg yolks, ½ cup of the sugar, and the salt in the bowl of an electric mixer (or use a large mixing bowl and an electric whisk) and beat until pale and mousselike—about 5 minutes. Mash and stir the chestnut purée with the back of a spoon in a small bowl, to break it up a bit, then whisk it into the egg-yolk mixture.

In a large, scrupulously clean bowl and using clean beaters, whisk the egg whites until they form stiff peaks. Add the remaining sugar to the egg whites, a quarter at a time, whisking after each addition.

Using a large metal spoon, carefully fold the melted chocolate mixture into the egg-yolk mixture. Finally, fold in the beaten egg whites. Be as gentle as you can so that you keep as much air in the mixture as possible.

Pour the batter into the prepared pan and bake in the preheated oven for 40–45 minutes, or until well risen. Let cool in the pan. It will sink in the middle as it does so, but this is normal.

Transfer the pan to a large serving plate or cutting board and release the side clip. Lift the ring from the torte and carefully slide the cake off the bottom, using a spatula or fish slice. Peel off the parchment paper. Dust the torte lightly with cocoa powder and scatter the chopped hazelnuts over the top.

apple, rum, and raisin cupcakes

These are cupcakes with a difference—they contain all the flavors of a Caribbean rum punch: dark rum, spices, and fruit.

⅔ cup raisins

2 tablespoons dark rum

10 tablespoons butter, softened and cubed

¾ cup light muscovado or packed light brown sugar

2 large eggs, lightly beaten

1⅙ cups self-rising flour, sifted

generous fresh grating of nutmeg

2 apples

1 ripe banana

finely grated peel of 1 orange

Icing

½ cup confectioners' sugar

½ teaspoon freshly grated nutmeg, plus extra for sprinkling

1 teaspoon dark rum

3–4 teaspoons freshly squeezed orange juice

a 12-cup muffin pan, lined with paper cupcake liners

Makes 12

Preheat the oven to 350°F.

Tip the raisins into a small bowl with the rum, stir, and set aside while you make the rest of the batter.

Put the butter, sugar, beaten eggs, flour, and grated nutmeg in an electric mixer (or use a large mixing bowl and an electric whisk). Whisk together to combine.

Core, peel, and chop the apples into small pieces. Peel and chop the banana into small pieces too and stir into the cake batter with the apples, three-quarters of the orange peel, and all the soaked raisins and rum.

Spoon the batter into the cupcake liners. Bake in the preheated oven for 25–30 minutes, or until risen and golden. Let cool on a wire rack.

When you are ready to ice the cupcakes, sift the confectioners' sugar into a small bowl and stir in the grated nutmeg. Add the rum, then the orange juice, a teaspoon at a time, stirring between each addition —you may not need it all. Spoon the icing over the cupakes and sprinkle a little extra nutmeg and the remaining grated orange peel over each one. Let set before serving.

brown sugar pavlova with cinnamon cream and pomegranate

This is a perfect winter party piece. In the summer, top the meringue with summer berries or a mixture of sliced peaches or nectarines and blueberries instead.

4 large egg whites

¼ cup light muscovado sugar

generous ¾ cup sugar (unrefined cane sugar is best here)

1 teaspoon cornstarch

1 teaspoon white wine vinegar

1¼ cups heavy or whipping cream

1 tablespoon confectioners' sugar

1½ teaspoons ground cinnamon

¾–1 cup pomegranate seeds

a baking sheet, lined with baking parchment (don't grease it, or your egg whites will collapse!)

Serves 8

Preheat the oven to 275°F.

Put the egg whites in a large, scrupulously clean bowl and whisk with an electric whisk (or use an electric mixer) until they form stiff peaks. Add the sugars, a tablespoon at a time, whisking constantly. Add the cornstarch and vinegar with the final addition of sugar.

Pile the meringue mixture onto the prepared baking sheet and form into a circle about 9 inches in diameter. Make swirls in the meringue with a skewer or the end of a teaspoon. Bake in the preheated oven for 1 hour, then turn the oven off and leave the pavlova in until cold — overnight is ideal.

To finish, whip the cream with the confectioners' sugar and cinnamon to soft peaks. Pile it onto the pavlova and scatter the pomegranate seeds over the top.